THESE THREE REMAIN

A COLLECTION OF ESSAYS EXPLORING FAITH IN QUESTIONS, HOPE IN STRUGGLE, AND LOVE IN AN ORDINARY LIFE

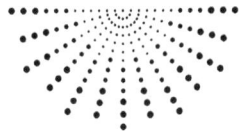

MICHELLE HURST

Copyright © 2025 Starfish Stories Publishing LLC.

Library and Archives Canada Cataloguing in Publications.

Copyright in Ontario, Canada and Lake Worth, Florida.

All rights reserved.

No part of this book may be reproduced in any form or by any electronic or mechanical means, including information storage and retrieval systems, without written permission from the author, except for the use of brief quotations in a book review.

NO Generative Artificial Intelligence (AI) was used in the writing of this work. Without in any way limiting Michelle Hurst (the author) and Starfish Stories Publishing LLC.'s exclusive rights under copyright, any use of this publication to "train" generative artificial intelligence (AI) technologies to generate text or for any other purpose is expressly prohibited.

For permissions contact:

hello@starfishstoriespublishing.com

E-Book ISBN: 978-1-990419-54-6

Paperback ISBN: 978-1-990419-53-9

Hardcover ISBN: 978-1-990419-55-3

1st Edition

Some names and details have been changed to protect privacy.

Edited by: C.B. Moore

Cover curated by: Starfish Indie Author Services

To Shaun, my solid and steady partner;
To Owen, my smart and tender joy;
And to Tess, my stubborn and fierce inspiration.
Loving and being loved by you is the reason I have any words to write.

DIGITAL ACCOMPANYING STUDY
GUIDE

Grab the digital accompanying study guide for free right here:

PREFACE

A slightly younger me was naive enough to think that tough seasons would sharpen my faith and strengthen my relationships. I had heard this in testimonies, read it in books. Refiner's fire and all that. Surely God would work together all things for good, but that was before.

More than once, I have heard a speaker talk on 1 Corinthians 13. As a college student, one minister asked us to write our name each time in place of the word love. Michelle is patient. Michelle is kind. Michelle does not envy, she does not boast.

Blasphemy in every line. It is an honorable enough goal, but one like everything else in my faith that I could never live up to.

Instead, I used it as a litmus test for relationships. A truer picture of what love should look like than I knew before. But after twenty-three years of marriage, I can promise you that sometimes love loses her patience. Sometimes love is crabby. Sometimes love is jealous. But love still chooses something bigger than herself over and over and over. Be it a marriage or motherhood or her faith.

Later the passage gets harder. Paul makes a tough promise to keep. Love never fails.

PREFACE

I believed this in my twenties. Marriage was always forever. God makes hard things good and peaceful. Now, decades later, I feel differently. There is so much overwhelming evidence that makes me question these platitudes and promises.

Paul, wiser than me, keeps going. Often in scripture and life and a good story we stop too early. Here Paul adds his caveat, he reminds us that we don't have the whole picture. For now, we only see a little bit. Paul promises that eventually we will know fully and sometimes peace and understanding come later. Much later. Some days it feels awfully hard to wait. I want to be known fully and loved anyways. I want peace and patience and a love that never fails instead of one that occasionally falls short or feels alone or is running late. On this side of things, even if you are only half-known, even if you are looking through a broken reflection, even if we only get the half of it, the verse ends with a promise that I have learned the hard way not to question: these three remain. I thought I knew, but I didn't really know it until everything else didn't work. Until a refining.

I've had a few before and afters. A few fires: chronic pain, illness, loss and a never-ending grief. Afters can wreck you because they seem to shake and test everything you are leaning on. One commonality for me is that they make me question my befores. They pull back just enough to remind me of everything I don't know and cannot control.

A few years ago, my mother, who has always been anxious and tightly wound, but never had any mental health issues, was suddenly in complete psychosis. We had no idea why and were not prepared for how hard it would be for her to receive care. She was too physically healthy for the hospital to treat her and too old for most behavioral health places to take her. We were lost. Over the course of a few months, I drove the three hours home again and again, and eventually walked into a scene that reminded me that sometimes it takes losing everything to see what remains.

My father prides himself on a large dining room table; he wants a space large enough for us all to gather and fills it as often as he can with pies and people, but on this day the table is cluttered only with dozens of prescription bottles. Multiple copies of a medical power of attorney. I sit and start to dig through papers and medical discharge forms that do not tell me enough. They offer a description of symptoms but no way forward, buried in a weeks' worth of newspapers, bills, junk mail and xeroxed recipes.

In my attempt to make stacks and sense of things, I see my dad's legal pad. His hard-to-read but easy to recognize tick marks down the page. It is next to the adding machine. Old school. My heart sags when I see what he has done. My father has spent over fifty years as a CPA. He is recently retired, but fifty years of bottom lines, audits, adding machine tape and balance sheets are a hard habit to break. In crisis, my dad went back to the comfort of numbers. Down an entire page and partway through a second, he has tallied and added up every single account and asset. The total at the bottom is staggering to me. But. It. Isn't. Enough. Savings, properties, insurance, 401Ks. They can't always fix what is broken.

We go back and forth to the hospital for days. They won't check her in, but there isn't anywhere for her to go either, so they shuffle her around in the ER. We ignore the one-person-a day visitation policy and go in and out at our leisure. I run to CVS, Target, and for food over and over again. My dad tells the nurses, doctor, and anyone who will listen that his two daughters are doctors. He doesn't mention that my degree is in education. Still, titles and education don't seem to matter here either. This is their third trip to this hospital in a month. (And there will be another.) He keeps coming back to this one because he used to serve on the board. He tries dropping names. A decade ago, they might have recognized him, but not now.

I'm not sure it would have mattered. He calls doctors, lawyers, and even his congressman. I ask to speak to a social worker or for any kind of number to call. We gain no ground.

PREFACE

No one is more prepared for aging and death than my parents. At least on the practical business end of things. They have purchased plots, picked out hymns, and given us their preferences. My siblings and I all have copies of power of attorney, wills (living and afterwards).

There are advance directives, insurance, co-insurance, and insurance for assisted living.

We have access to the safe, safety deposit box, and can all sign on the checking account.

We know that it is an even split. We know the names of the lawyer, the doctor, and even the vet.

They've started giving away things: furniture, appliances, jewelry, tools.

But we were not prepared for this. In this particular season, the things I was taught were so important suddenly do not help.

Money. Education. Prominence. Preparation.

Turns out, when it comes down to it, none of those things matter as much as we think they do. The bottom line on my father's ledger doesn't match our hearts. We are at a loss, empty and unsure of next steps. Of what the future might be. If there is one. If we even want it. We are wrecked, lost and desperate.

A few days later, with a little bit of rest and a few narrow paths forward, I wonder what actually does matter if all those promises do not. So I make a list, and it isn't terribly long, but I think it covers plenty of ground.

Showing up.

People that feed my family while I'm gone.

A husband who is a true partner.

The kindness of others.

Prayers, mostly other people's because in this season I don't trust my own.

A God who doesn't always show up, but I still believe is good.

A family that doesn't always agree but manages to work together.

PREFACE

When money, education and prominence don't get you anywhere, I'm left with these three things:

Stubborn faith.

Reckless hope.

Plain and ordinary love.

Even weeks later, still in almost the same uncertainty, when the system has failed us, those three are enough. Some seasons I have held tightly to my faith, but in this one it has held tightly to me. This season has required me to let go of many things. But these three remain.

They have held, and I have held them.

When I really think about it, I have a hard time distinguishing those three words: faith, hope, and love. They are easily confused and not always religious. For me, it boils down to this: faith is belief, hope is expectation, and love is acceptance. I've found them in church pews, on hiking trails, in hospital hallways, on dusty hilltops and cold green rivers. Or maybe I should say they've found me. My faith is a question where the answer matters less than the asking. My hope is a scar. A mark that doesn't go away even when the pain does. Love is what I am learning to sit in and accept and give freely.

I still believe in that promise of Romans 8_1, but I now know that God working things together for the good can first feel like heartbreak. Maybe some of you have found peace in your hardest moments; instead, I have found questions, anguish, and exhaustion.

The peace came eventually. Much later. Possibly because I wanted God to show up differently. I wanted a God to help me skip through the hard parts or to make them feel less hard. I wanted refining without the flame. For almost a decade I have lived with a chronic-pain condition. I know a few things about managing pain, and I think I wanted God to lessen the pain. I have leaned on my faith, but also my abilities. Only one of those survived the fire. My God is not a pill to ease my symptoms, instead I have just had to lean into them. Sometimes I could feel His presence. Sometimes I just

PREFACE

hoped for it. Sometimes I couldn't do either. Sometimes our pain isn't less, but we are never alone in it. We aren't even alone in feeling alone in it.

That is the stubborn faith. That is the reckless hope. That is the love that doesn't fail.

PART I
STUBBORN FAITH

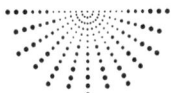

"Acknowledging uncertainty doesn't make a person less faithful; it just makes her more honest. Admitting how much we don't know doesn't make a person less faithful; it just makes him more candid — and perhaps more curious. Anne Lamott has chronicled the meanderings of the heart as well as anyone, and as she famously puts it, 'The opposite of faith is not doubt, but certainty.'"
—— **Rachel Held Evans**

ME OF LITTLE FAITH

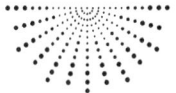

I HAVE ALWAYS GIVEN MY KIDS FREE REIN IN THE KITCHEN. Despite the messes, I figure it is a safe place for them to problem-solve, and I occasionally get cookies out of the deal.

When she was young, my daughter attempted to make a cake, and we had most of the ingredients. In baking, close enough rarely works out. My daughter has watched me cook meals for years. I rarely use a recipe; I swap ingredients out I don't like or don't have, and I always add more garlic or cheese than necessary. This works for most entrees and sauces, but my willy-nilly approach does not work for cookies or cakes. My daughter carefully followed the directions on the box, she measured ingredients (at least the ones we did have), stirred and mixed. She added a little extra oil since we did not have an egg. It looked like a normal baking mix going into the perfectly preheated oven, but it came out looking more like a yellow brick than a fluffy cake. She had been missing a vital ingredient, and the result was not worth saving, even with extra frosting.

I've often wondered if I have been missing a necessary ingredient when it comes to faith. I wish there was a recipe to follow (not that

I'd follow it, but at least I could tell you where I went wrong). Instead, we are all making it up. I may struggle to follow directions for baking, but I have certainly attempted to follow all the rules for religion. Generally, those prescriptive models have never tasted right to me. My heart has occasionally felt more brick than tender. I've been struggling and substituting and never end up with what I think faith should look like. Something has always been missing, this part of me that everyone else seemed to have. The vital missing ingredient: a solid belief or innate goodness. A few times in my life, I have been desperate for that kind of faith and steadiness. At other times, I have been equally desperate to shake it. To cast my faith aside. To slip it off like jeans that no longer fit. However, my faith has never given me a constant assurance nor the ability to leave it.

It is equal parts slippery and clingy. Hebrews 11_2 describes faith as "assurance in things hoped for, assurance of things not seen," which feels like a pretty tall order. My faith has always had a side of doubt and a belief that has firmly held on to me rather than the other way around. I've wanted a know-it-in-my-bones feeling but have carried around more of the "I sure as hell hope it is true" variety. As for things unseen, I've always needed my faith to have a physicality to it. I need to taste the bread and the wine. I need to feel the hard pews. I need to hear the hymns and smell the river water. I need a faith that can be touched and held and wrestled with and counted on.

I am not much of a public crier, even when I should be, yet my eyes flood at every baptism, marriage and funeral I attend. I am not a particularly holy person. I swear. I drink too much. I am selfish and can eat my weight in chips and salsa, but I long for holy moments and spaces. I cannot remember my own baptism. I was a baby in a hand-me-down white gown. My own children were twelve when they were dunked in a river on unusually cold days in April. I wept and shivered. Spirituality to me is too abstract. I need cold water, ashes, wedding cake and funeral processions to draw out my faith. To pull the emotions down my cheeks. To remind me that God is there in the beginning, in the good and in the fullness and emptiness and grief.

My faith used to feel so much bigger. These days it can feel like an afterthought. A prayer shot off in traffic or as I am already falling asleep. I struggle through any kind of devotional book. I make it to church most weekends but pray with my eyes open and occasionally with my heart closed. I still talk to my God all the time in ways that seem too honest to call prayer. Sometimes I feel like it is a one-sided conversation, but I can't seem to hang up.

Twenty years ago, my faith took up so much more space. There were Christian CDs mixed in with the ones marked "explicit lyrics." There was usually beer in my fridge and always a Bible on my coffee table. I hung out in coffee shops, college ministries and apartment hot tubs.

I made all the mistakes, but I still managed to squeeze in a quiet time or go to a Bible study.

We wrote our requests on notecards and traded them like baseball cards and taped them to our bathroom mirrors. We muttered long, exhausting prayers about things I wouldn't spend two minutes on now. Even then, my faith never felt as solid as I thought everyone else's must have.

It felt slippery and loose and full of gray, like I must be doing it wrong. Yet, somehow, it also felt warm and big and true.

I miss it. This small narrow faith that felt so consuming. It filled living room couches and strummed guitars. It had hands to hold during ridiculous prayers. I still fill my kitchen and wine glasses and keep a guitar gathering dust in the corner. My daughter only occasionally lets me hold her hand. There are books littering my coffee table, but it would take me a few minutes to locate a Bible. Crosses hang on my wall. I still make it to church more Sundays than not.

My faith still feels slippery and loose and full of gray, but these days I think that maybe that means that I am doing it right. I go in circles of chasing it and being chased.

In our current context, faith, at least a Christian one, can be associated with an expected political view or intolerance I don't agree with. Faith was never meant to be a political party. In something that is defined by assurance, how do you incorporate nuance? How does it become an "and" rather than an excluder? I used to be jealous of the people that I thought had such a solid faith. Now I'm embarrassed by them. I wanted a deep-seated belief that they never seem to question or wrestle. But maybe the questions and the wrestling are what make a faith softer and allows it to expand and include. A faith that bends can also encircle. It becomes a soft place to land rather than a hard stone in my chest. And since we are being honest, faith doesn't always work, at least not the way I want it to.

Because what happens when He doesn't come through? What if the check doesn't come?

Or the test results are not what you hoped for? Or when the phone rings in the middle of the night? Or when your friend is never coming back? Where does that leave my faith or my God?

Is it big enough to still believe in after those kinds of hits?

"If you have faith as small as a mustard seed, you can say to this mulberry tree, 'Be uprooted and planted in the sea,' and it will obey you." Luke 17:6 (NIV).

The expectation has never been a big giant faith. Only a tiny one. A smidge. A seed.

I was never missing a solid faith; instead, I was lucky to have grown a stubborn one, like a pebble or a seed stuck in my shoe. Insisting on being felt, even when I try my best to ignore it and power onward. My stubborn little faith, reminding me it is still there. Sometimes even annoyingly so. When my journey is filled with hard and doubt and hustle.

A small seed pressing. A reminder.

I will not leave you.

My stubborn faith is teaching me that it has never been a recipe to follow. There are no essential ingredients, despite what any three-point sermon or spiritual book may try to tell me. I'm not baking a cake. I'm learning to love and be loved. I'm hoping it turns out OK, but the beauty is that God uses both bricks and cakes to build his kingdom and feed his people. I can't screw it up. So use whatever you have. It only takes a little bit.

RIVERS, LAKES AND OCEANS

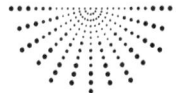

My husband and his family are mountain people. They can fish and sit on the back porch for weeks and not ever want to go anywhere. Each summer we spend a week in the mountains, and I can see the appeal. I like the way the air tastes cleaner. I love the grand views, the fact that it isn't 110 degrees (like at home) and that you can see a billion stars.

My family of origin, however, spends a week each summer at the beach. The second we cross the long bridge from the mainland and I breathe in the salty air. It isn't like the mountains. It is loud. The waves and the city. Everything feels thick and sweaty. The sand gets in absolutely everything, but there is no doubt that I come from the water.

Rivers

I was baptized in the Guadalupe. Not officially. I'm sure that happened before I can remember in a church. A sprinkle of water from the hand of a pastor. A promise meant for me to unpack later

— a promise I'm still untangling. But in the river I was baptized, not of my faith, but of myself.

I spent the almost entire month of July plunging in the dark earthy water, most summers from age ten to twenty-two. July after July, on those banks and in those waters, I learned how to be comfortable as myself. I didn't have to try too hard or feel like too much. I didn't have to impress or make myself smaller. I showed up, jumped in, and bathed in acceptance, wantedness, and community. I carried that with me the other eleven months of the year. We lounged at free swim and then lined up for a lifeguard to drop alcohol in our ears. We ripped the bottoms out of our bathing suits sliding down the rapids. We jumped off the dam when we were supposed to be fishing and intentionally flipped our canoes.

The water was always cold, green, and smelled dark and earthy. It was too deep to touch bottom and few of us were brave enough to swim the extra few feet down, algae tickling our legs. Years later, when I returned as summer staff, we'd buy inner tubes and float less visible parts of the river with beers we were not old enough to buy. I'd once summon all courage and throw myself off the 1340 bridge into the water below.

Baptism is supposed to be a declaration of belief. A confession of faith. A symbol of death and resurrection. A washing away of sin. I won't pretend to have any of that symbolism here. The river may not have washed me clean, but it always held me up. It always reminded me of who I was. I returned year after year. July after July after July.

On Sundays we slept late. We did not circle around the flag and trek across the catwalk to the dining hall for runny eggs or greasy bacon. Instead, we wandered down the stairs of our dorm to the tiny kitchen and grabbed cereal or pastries. Most of us still in pajamas, with our hair wild and smelling of campfire, we ate on the back porch or front steps. Someone always forgot and let the screen doors slam. After picking all the marshmallows out of our Lucky Charms, we eventually went back inside, each of us digging to the bottom of our footlockers, looking for our Sunday uniforms. On competition nights, we wore our team colors and painted our faces, but on Sundays we all dressed the same — everyone wore white. We hated our Sunday whites; they were usually dirty before we made it up the hill. The hilliest of hills in all of Hill Country. I feel like it was miles to the top, but I suspect it was only a ten-minute hike. We complained the whole way up.

Chapel on the hill was always different from the rest of the week. Often there would be a a guest preacher, but eighty or so girls aged eight to college paid no attention to the pastor. We were hot. The stone seats were uncomfortable. We sang. We watched the birds fly below us. We braided each other's hair. The fourth and final Sundays had our parents behind us, waiting patiently to take photos from the top with the river winding below us. I do not remember any special words or sermons or prayers. Our shoes were covered in dust, our butts hurt. Sweat stained the armpits of our white button ups. After church, we flew down the hill. Without fail, someone would scrape a leg or sprain an ankle. We dropped our already dirty whites in the laundry hoping they would get clean by next Sunday and slipped on our swimsuits and clothes that were more comfortable and less likely to stain. We ate lunch or dinner at the river rather than the dining hall. There were no classes. Only chapel on the hill and the river. They were my favorite days.

I suspect, however, that most girls who spent their Sundays at the top of the hill like me will tell you it is holy ground. That if they go back to visit, every single one would make the hike up the hill. The property is over five-hundred acres, with all kinds of amenities and special places. Yet every one of us who goes back to visit climbs the hill. We don't drive up. We park at the dorm and walk. Just like we did at ten and fifteen and twenty.

I have only been back a few times since my twenties but can still picture it perfectly in my head. I'd make my way up the hill. I would find a stone bench, if I'm lucky — one with a little bit of shade and a full view of the valley below. This is the place where no one would care if tears fell. And after, I'd walk down, past the dorm. Over the catwalk. Past the tennis courts and the river dorms. Past the dam, and straight to the water. I'd return again.

Clean. Free. Alive. Safe. Buoyed up. Baptized.

Ponds, Lakes and Bays

I must come by this desire to be near the water naturally. When I was young, we would drive out to the country. Someone would let me drive in the deep rutted gravel roads, long before I could reach the pedals. We'd pick dewberries in May and someone would always fish. I'd throw my line in too, but usually get too distracted by the cows or grasshoppers or anything beyond the tank dam to stay in my lawn chair for long.

My parents eventually sold their place in the country and bought a sailboat. We spent every weekend in Kemah and out on the Galveston Bay. Then they sold the boat and bought a condo on Lake Conroe. Then another sailboat. Then a bigger place on the lake. There has always been water. Ponds. Bays. Lakes. It didn't matter. Each week my father would escape the demands of his work to some form of water. We'd fish, skip rocks, trim the sails or bounce in a tube behind a pontoon boat.

My own children only know the lake. When I visit, I often have to resist walking straight onto the dock to lie down flat. Instead, I bring in my bags, hug hello, and make conversation inside all while my son rigs his fishing pole. Eventually, I make my way to the wood. Most people just sit on the dock and let their feet dangle. I need full contact. I need to feel my back on the warm planks. To hear the waves gently breaking on almost every side.

It is what I think about in the middle of nights far from the water as I am trying desperately to find a way back to sleep in the 3 a.m. hours. I try to remember this. The hot humid air. The gentle water.

The quiet water lapping against the dock. My body rooted somewhere in between.

We visited the lake often during COVID. For a few months, we were all forced to work and attend school from home, so why not do it somewhere with a better view? The world seemed to be falling apart, and I found my way to the water. The lake house is in an area called Walden, even though there is a giant lake in lieu of a pond. They have had this house for over a decade, but I can still get lost in the neighborhoods. More often than not, that is even the goal. Each night I'd walk new streets and my daughter, Tess, would often join me. We'd wander all the way down the trail. I'd lose count of the deer who didn't seem fazed by the humans in their woods. I listened to the quiet crunch of gravel beneath our shoes as she talked incessantly. She was way too old, but once or twice I'd try to hold her hand. Begging for something to hold me here, pulling me back to something solid; for something to help keep my mind in place — and she occasionally obliged, but only for a moment.

Those days and honors must have passed, unannounced like most little moments of childhood. No one tells you that the firsts are photographed and celebrated, but what you long for is for someone to warn you about the lasts. The last time your child let you walk them into school or a party unembarrassed. The last time they said Momma instead of just a flat Mom. I want to be told so I can let those moments be soaked in and remembered. Not to just slip so loosely away that we don't even notice until after they are gone. I feel that I am in a different season of lasts. Ones where I am the child and the parent at the same time.

After our walks and after the sun disappears, I steal the blanket off the couch, wrap it around me and lie back on the dock. No one seems to be out. It is just me, the stars, and the water. So much has changed so quickly. The dynamics and rules of our world, work and even our family completely shifted in such a short season. My balance thrown.

The only way I know to restore it is to lie flat on a dock. And listen to the quiet water breaking.

Water has to find balance. It can't do anything else. The right amount of flow in and out of a system. Always seeking an even level. I try so hard to hope for the same things, all with a loss and ache and the beginnings of hope in my chest.

Oceans

Almost every summer, my extended family goes to the beach. It is usually a close Texas beach, but we have occasionally ventured farther. We've had perfect weather and hit the same time as tropical storms. We've had white sands and seaweed-covered ones. We've had fancy dinners and beach boils. We've burned and brawled and boogie-boarded.

When I was small, I'd order a dozen oysters on the half shell and the servers would come watch me eat them in disbelief. To me, they taste like the ocean, and more than once I've found a pearl. Each trip, even when I don't order oysters, I look for the pearl.

Last trip, it rained almost every day, but each day when the sun came out (or even occasionally when it didn't) we'd find our way to the sand. We ran, played bocce and kubb, hunted for crabs and body-surfed in our small pockets of sunshine. We all grew more freckles, got salt in our eyes, and sand in between our toes and in our swimsuits. Unlike at the lake, the water isn't quiet. It is a loud roar you can hear even from the very top-floor balcony. Sometimes I need the quiet to find my own stillness, but at the beach I love the loudness. The vastness of an ocean filling all my senses: the sharp tang of salt, seaweed and fish, the grit of sand, the burning of my shoulders no matter how much sunscreen I put on, and an ocean roar that fills my head so much that I can't hear all the noise that often takes up almost the whole real estate. All I hear are the waves.

I wade past the sandbar, and the waves nearly knock me over.

The rip current pulls at my feet. I look out my window and the ocean seems to go on forever. There is nothing that should be peace-giving about the ocean — but somehow it is.

When I go to the mountains, I want to hike for miles and miles; when I am at the ocean, I want to walk along the shore until it ends. I walked until I ran out of beach, until I was surrounded on three sides by water. My own children are lucky enough to get both each summer: a mountaintop and an ocean. People often talk about mountaintop experiences. I've been on my share of mountain tops, and it is hard to NOT to be moved by God's beauty from such great heights, but the ocean is different. Oceans are usually at the lowest elevations and maybe why what Paul wrote in Ephesians speaks to me more at my lowest points:

"How long, how wide, how deep, and how high his love really is; and to experience this love for yourselves, though it is so great that you will never see the end of it or fully know or understand it. And so at last you will be filled up with God himself."

The ocean meets us at our lowest points. It isn't subtle or majestic. There is no wide lens view — all you can see is the water. It is vast and loud and gritty and harsh, but it is deep and wide and fills us up. It gets between our toes. It drowns out the noise. It crashes over us. Again and again and again.

I've heard that there are few things in life that salt water can't cure: sweat, tears or the ocean. Water doesn't fix all things; it can't touch disease or pain or repair relationships, but it can offer a respite. It can offer a baptism, a leveling and pockets of sunshine when everything else feels overcast. It is quiet and calm, or loud enough to cancel out the rest of the noise. It takes grit and makes a pearl. For me, it has always been a place to become, to return and to try again.

This year we stopped on the way to the beach to take our son on a college tour, and my parents only shuffled onto the sand once all week. It is not lost on me that these trips may be nearing a close. Our family dynamics can be complicated. There are a lot of us, and we land all over the map on opinions and politics. We are impatient and loud. Author Jen Hatmaker likes to say that some families are sweet and others are spicy. Well, ours isn't sweet or spicy — I'd say we are salty, and not just with our language. Sometimes our worst comes out at the beach, but it is still a place we return to each year to try again to be our best. Each year, we order more wine, we fill a long table, we miss those who aren't with us, and we toast to another year.

SUNDAYS

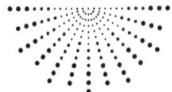

Many of my Sunday nights are spent with high school youth at my church. Last month the theme was testimonies. Each week a speaker shared their story. I read hundreds of books. I write my own stories and publish them publicly, but I've never written one in the form of a testimony. When the youth director announced the theme and led with a graphic of befores and afters, I hesitated.

Suddenly I was back in college, eagerly eating salad at Olive Garden. A friend's mom was in town and offered to take a few of us out to dinner. I was thrilled to eat anywhere other than the dining hall until she asked, ever so casually, when each of us had "been saved." I almost choked on my breadstick. I grew up going to church, but this was not the kind of question my family dropped around the dinner table. At that moment, the only thing I wanted to be saved from was our dinner conversation.

Still, I knew how to answer the way I thought she wanted. I told her about a night at a church camp. One with a band and an altar call when I made my way up to the front. It was all true, but it wasn't necessary. It wasn't like I didn't know Jesus before that, and I don't really think I needed to say the sinner's prayer to secure my place in heaven. Maybe that works, but I think a hundred other prayers will do the trick.

Back to Sunday nights: each week a new speaker shared and gave assurance that all our stories mattered. Even ones that weren't dramatic. Even if you couldn't really remember a before. Still, this theme had me thinking how I'd answer that question without the promise of unlimited salad and breadsticks. I hunted down my high school yearbook and turned to my picture. The girl in the photo was full of contradictions. I cared a lot about what I wore and how my hair looked. I cared about my grades. I cared about what boys said hi to me in the hallways. I cared more about those things than my own heart. Yet I spent a good chunk of my time pretending that I didn't care about anything. My faith was black and white. Good and bad. In or out. I bought CDs with explicit lyrics, and I threw them away. I made promises and I broke them. On the surface I had success, good grades, friends, dates to dances and drawers full of awards, but I was also lonely. I felt unwanted. I more than felt it. I lived it. I felt like my faith mattered, but I also felt like I must be missing something that everyone else seemed to have: assurance. They trusted what I questioned. Faith seemed easier for everyone else. They prayed; my mind wandered. They resisted; I stumbled. They were made for a relationship; I was constantly battling them. I wanted to be good, but I also wanted to be liked. I knew the right answers, but I didn't always know how to feel them.

When we would get our yearbooks, one of the first things I'd do each year was flip to the index in the back and find my name. I'd go to each page listed and look at the pictures. Then I'd do the same for guys I was crushing on. Our yearbook did a good job of trying to balance coverage, but still some people showed up more than others. A goal I had my senior year was for that space after my name in the index to take up more than one line. I wanted to be in the yearbook so much that it took two lines to list all the pages I'd be on. This wasn't a goal I wrote down anywhere, but I wasn't quiet about it. And like most goals I set then and now, I met it.

I still want those things; I was just never going to find it in my high school yearbook.

Back then we did not have social media to measure our worth, so instead I used the index. I'm embarrassed to think about it. It wasn't that I wanted to be in the yearbook so badly, but that

I wanted badly to be seen. To be included. I wanted evidence that I mattered.

I THINK at sixteen I assumed that eventually I'd grow up and figure it all out. I imagined this knowledge was gifted to you around twenty-two, with a college degree, and if you were lucky a husband. I thought that I would stop feeling lonely, even in a crowded room. I thought that faith would be easier. I thought I'd stop striving to be seen.

I was wrong. The contradictions have followed me into adulthood.

A faith testimony is supposed to have three basic parts: a description of your life before, the turning point and a description of changes made and life after. But I think we screw this up. We want it to be dramatic. At sixteen (and occasionally now), I had plenty of dramatic moments. Jesus, however, was steady even when I wasn't. I don't think I can provide those three parts of testimony. There are plenty of biblical examples. Burning bushes, floods, a blind man on an ass, and a thief on a cross. There was certainly an after for each — but I wouldn't say was always an appealing one.

Plagues, ridicule, the worst cruise ever, prison, and death.

My story is mostly just a "during."

Recently I took an online class on personal essays. The facilitator told us that all good essays have to do two things: they answer a question and they show transformation.

The questions are always changing:
What is the next right thing?
Where am I supposed to be?
What is my hope really?
Is God good?
Does he care about me, specifically?

Which sounds a lot like my yearbook quest — Does He see me? Am I doing enough?

That moment when someone awkwardly asked me about my testimony at dinner wasn't the answer to any of those questions. Actually, I'd grow up and live into a hundred more. I'm in my mid-forties, and sometimes I still feel lonely and left out.

Sometimes I wish my faith was easier.

Sometimes I still strive to be seen.

If that was all you knew, my before would look uncomfortably close to my after.

However, I'd say those questions are less befores and mostly the things that make me human.

As for transformations, in almost all the example essays we read the changes were not dramatic. They were small and subtle rather than giant awakenings. Acceptance and the courage to take the next steps. What if my testimony is less of a before and after story and more of a collection of essays? A small part of something that is much bigger. Room for more questions and subtle transformations. Something that grows and shifts and changes. A forever during, rather than a single before and after.

I started writing some of my stories online in 2007, which means there are many years' worth of essays I can go back and compare to now. On occasion, I go back and read my writing. One of a few things always happens: I cringe at both my abilities and some of the content.

Sometimes I wrote exactly what future me needed to hear.

Sometimes I hate that I'm still struggling with the exact same things.

Sometimes I have a whole lot more compassion for past me.

My old essays are a hint at before and after and during. Every time I cringe it is because I've grown, either as a writer or a person (usually both). My essays over time make room for that change and growth, even if the themes often don't always change. Room for gray and growth rather than the rigid black-and-white faith that often pulled teenagers down the center aisle. Not a before and after but an ongoing pursuit and examination. A during may feel less compelling, less dramatic. But you'd be wrong. I'd still have plenty of advice for my sixteen-year-old self. I may still carry many of the same questions and aches, but I think we all do. The contradictions I felt at sixteen give way to an adult who can hold space for the paradox and mystery that a life of faith requires. The yoke is easy and the burden is light, but sometimes our hearts are still heavy. The difference isn't that I suddenly have answers, it is that I have more information. More specifically, I have a hope and assurance that I was still trying to figure out at sixteen. A hope and assurance that I'm still growing at forty-five. I'm still in the middle of it.

The middle has a few things I want the sixteen-year-old me and the sixteen-year-olds that show up each Sunday to know:

You may occasionally feel lonely, but you aren't alone.

You may wish your faith was easier. It never gets easy, but it does hold. Sometimes you will hold tightly to your faith and other times it will hold tightly to you.

Not everyone will see you or want you, but the God of the universe who counts and names the stars also knows the number of hairs on my head. She sees each freckle and fear and question. My name may be listed over and over in the back of the yearbook, but more importantly it is engraved on the palms of the God's hands.

One last thing, I'd tell that sixteen-year-old: eat ALL the breadsticks. Teenage metabolism doesn't last.

PRAYER

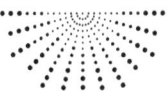

It was late and I'd already tucked in my son once and then re-tucked him in after he got up the first time. I should have already been in bed, but once again I found myself sitting on the couch scrolling, watching late night TV and wasting time.

When he called for me a third time, I gave up. I shut down the computer and crawled into his twin-sized bed. I let his buzzed hair tickle my chin while I kissed the top of his head and asked what was wrong. He said that he was scared and that he didn't want to sleep in this tiny bed all alone. He explained that I got to sleep with Dad every night, and couldn't I just sleep with him for a little while? I assured him that his sister was right next door and that we were just down the hall. I suggested that he try and get the dog to sleep with him. He was not satisfied, and I was not willing to give up my queen-sized mattress for his twin-sized fear.

I reminded him that he was never really alone, and that when he gets scared he could always pray. Since prayer has always been elusive to grown-up me, and since he was only five, I asked him if he knew what it meant to pray. He had heard prayers often enough before bed or before dinner or at church, but I wasn't sure he really understood the concept. Sometimes I am not even sure I do.

My prayers[4] lately have mostly been "help" or "thank you," and I know all too well that sometimes it can just feel like a one-sided conversation. I worried for years that I was doing it wrong or not enough and hated having to pray out loud in front of others. The Psalms are my favorite model and permission to give God my unedited prayers since David wasn't afraid to cry out, complain, question or curse his enemies. I wasn't ready to teach my son to curse his enemies, but I did want him praying like David, with his whole heart.

My son stayed quiet, and I thought maybe he was already asleep, but I kept talking anyway. I told him that prayer was just talking to God. That He promises that when we call on Him, He will answer[5]. That he could pray whenever he wanted and say whatever he felt like. That there weren't any special rules or topics or things to memorize. Just talking, like to a friend. When he was scared or sad or thankful. I felt like my description fell a little flat but gave myself credit for trying.

I kissed his head again and got ready to sneak out of his room because he was still silent and breathing deep, and I thought surely he was already dreaming. Then ever so quietly he asked the question that plenty of grown-ups are too afraid to voice.

"But He never talks to me," he whispered.

I replied, "Of course He does. He just rarely uses out-loud words."

"But what does He sound like?"

I sighed. Because of course my tiny trusting son would ask the questions that still baffle me. "It is sometimes hard to tell, but He talks all the time. Mostly we just have to listen less with our ears and more with our hearts. He whispers in the wind. He fills in the quiet if we leave any room for Him. He sounds like a nagging feeling that won't go away. He sounds like laughter and extra scoops of ice cream and phrases in our favorite books. Sometimes He sounds an awful lot like other people, ones that we can hear just fine. And sometimes when we pray, He is quiet, sounding more like a hug feels."

Just then he wrapped his two little sleepy arms around me and squeezed me tight.

I whispered to him, "See, just then? I heard Him loud and clear."

STORE-BOUGHT

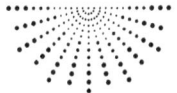

Many of the abstract parts of believing are difficult for me, but communion has always felt easy. Instead of quiet prayers or a long sermon, there is something to hold, smell, do, and taste. I love the physicality of it, whether I am given thimbles of grape juice and tasteless wafers or hunks of Hawaiian bread and goblets of wine. Communion has always been an invitation and a rare chance for me to press my knees into the cushion of the altar. It is not just the physical action but the singularity. A person at the front hands me a hunk of break and says, "This is Christ's body broken for you." Spoken just to me. Given just to me.

I'm not especially drawn to tradition or formalities. I prefer a church service with a guitar to an organ and I'd rather wear jeans than my Sunday best, but communion has always had a way of fixing what is broken inside me. I know different groups believe different things about what the bread and wine signify or what happens or who can take it. I don't care if it is a symbol or a mystery, I just like the chance to remember what Jesus did on his last night with his friends. To break bread is holy whether you do it at a table or an altar or your living room.

Christ did not only speak of the bread of life, but often of actual bread. Christ physically feeds the multitudes, he turns water into wine at a wedding, and he breaks bread with his friends. The metaphor doesn't work without the physicality, without the hungry hands accepting his gift. Maybe this is the reminder I need each time my church offers me communion. That faith is complicated and abstract, but also simple and can be held in my own hungry hands.

My particular church celebrates communion once a month and offers an open table where anyone is welcome to partake. This means that if my own children have made it all the way through the service, I take them with me. I know they don't know what it means, but I still bring them down the center aisle. I know many faith traditions have different conditions for communion, but I find hope in the fact that I don't have to completely understand it to accept the gift.

One communion Sunday, my son stopped coloring on the program long enough to listen to what the person at the front breaking bread was saying. The pastor explained what communion signifies and means as he ripped the round loaf in half. My son, only six but already a realist, said, "They just bought that at the store. It didn't come from God." Then repeated it in case we didn't hear, or in case the people in the pew behind us didn't hear. I laughed instead of sank. Maybe I shouldn't have, but his honesty stood out in a place where people often hide their questions and observations. I let my husband try to explain something about it being a symbol, which was far too much for his little head. He came to the altar with us anyway. Probably for a snack or the relief of not sitting still a few minutes, or maybe just to ask what store they'd bought it from. He stuck out his little hand and gladly took the bread from the store and the grape juice in the little cup from his friend's dad. He ate and drank and headed back to our pew to squirm and color on things that he shouldn't.

My son was correct in his statement: I'm sure they bought the bread at the store. I wondered for the first time if the church had a

Costco account. I'm pretty sure it is just King's Hawaiian bread and grape juice they buy in bulk. It made me wonder who provided the meal that night a long time ago, in the upper room. It was also just bread and wine in a cup and twelve friends around a table. Where the meal came from didn't matter. What made it important was who was there and the words that were said. What matters most is that He was willing to be broken and spilled out for them. And for me. Once a month, I tear off my piece of grocery store bread and drink my plastic thimbleful of grape juice and remember how ordinary things can become so holy.

PREACHERS AND PARADES

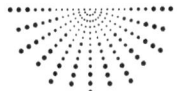

ONCE, I SAT IN A PEW AND TRIED TO NOT THINK ABOUT the fact that you could count on one hand the number of white congregants in the room. Me being one of the few. I did not want to draw attention to myself, but though I have been to church most Sundays of my life, I had no idea what to do. When to sit, stand, pray, or the lyrics to any of the songs. The rules here seemed so different than in my own church just a few miles away. Filled with people who mostly looked like me.

A few elderly African American women were seated next to me and were kind enough to attempt to make me feel welcome and tell me what to do. At some point Eunice, in a bright purple dress, slid her arthritic hand on top of mine, squeezed and tugged me to the front to pray.

I let her lead me because I didn't know how else to respond, and because she seemed so genuinely glad that I was there, singing off key next to her. It was not lost on me that my slight discomfort was one of choice and ended just as quickly as I got in my car and drove home. That discomfort is one most people, in that same sanctuary, probably feel all the time. I wondered how often they were one of the few people of color in a white sea. I wondered if there was anyone kind enough to take their hand, welcome them and patiently show them what to do.

Weeks later, some of my friends invited me to go to a Pride parade and join them giving out free mom hugs. Painting signs and making shirts of welcome and acceptance to a group that can often have strained relationships with their own parents. We hoped to be stand-ins.

We pulled up in a minivan. I looked more like I belonged on a Target aisle than at a Pride parade. I had not ordered a mom hug shirt, so I looked in my closet until I found some rainbow tie-dyed t-shirts in the back. We found a place along the parade route, right in front of a church that was doing it right — giving away water and opening its doors and restrooms.

The lawn was full of spectators dressed in all kinds of things and the fanciest of shoes. Music blared, drinks flowed, and I quickly started to sweat through my tie-dye. Even considering my long history with the Indigo Girls, I couldn't help but feel out of place. Like I didn't fit. Despite the fact that a guy behind me had on a blue wig, three-inch heels and fishnets, I felt that people were looking AT ME. Yet no one told me to leave, or questioned my morality, motives, or even my footwear.

Two college-age-looking girls to my left hesitantly wondered if it was really OK to ask for a hug. Another obnoxious guest, who had overserved herself and yelled in our ears, saw the signs and said she was likely almost the same age as us, but could really use a mom hug. We obliged.

There were plenty of hugs. Some shy. Some sweaty. More than a few with glitter. Some people literally ran to us with open arms and hearts. Kind of like Eunice's open hands.

I went to a Black church to learn and because I believe in unity (and for the music).

I went to the parade for many of the same reasons. In both places

I realized that I, in all my privilege, was suddenly the other. Even if only for a few hours. I stood out. I was uncomfortable. I wondered what people would think. I worried if it was OK to be tagged online.

I was only treated with love. Hugged a hundred times. Dragged to the altar. Welcomed and asked back by people who were not always treated as kindly by people like me; the same as me. That discomfort is not an easy outfit to put on, but it is an excellent teacher. And the best hugger and hand-holder I know.

LESS

LIKE MOST PEOPLE I SPEND A GOOD AMOUNT OF MY TIME trying to obtain things.
    More friends.
    More shoes.
    More confidence.
    More attention.
    More money.
    More followers.
    But the truth is I am much better at losing things.
    My keys.
    My ID.
    My wallet.
    My phone.
    My patience.
    My peace.
    Unless we are talking about weight, in most situations I'd rather gain than lose. Add more to my resumé or bookshelves than take away. Loss scares me. I hold on tightly to things, even ones that I know good and well I should loosen my grip on. I'd rather gain than

lose. Collect than release. I choose more over less almost every time. Except Jesus always flips the story. The last becomes first and less becomes more.

Creative work is often knowing when to stop. Rob Bell[6] reminds us that "Great artists know that it isn't just about what you add; sometimes the most important work is knowing what to take away. Removing clutter, excess, all the superfluous elements — and finding out in the process what's been in there the whole time."

A sculptor's entire job is to remove, to find a huge piece of stone or wood and make it less.

That the beauty is in there all along, and someone just has to take the time to carve it out.

To find it.

To free it.

To let everyone else see what lies underneath.

The same is true of writing. I start by getting it all down, but the real work comes from removing. By eliminating the words that get in the way and confuse, I make my message clearer. Editing involves looking at each sentence carefully and making sure that it's well designed and serves its purpose. Which sounds an awful like John 15:2, where Jesus tells us that "every branch that does bear fruit he prunes, that it may be even more fruitful." The dead and useless parts are cut away. We are made less so that we can be more.

Let's be honest. Most of us spend more time trying to cover up than we do revealing. We spend more time trying to become more rather than less. At least, I do. It is easier, safer and a whole lot less vulnerable. But more isn't art. It isn't beautiful. It makes for a confusing story and rarely bears fruit.

I do not know loss like some people I know.

I have never lost a parent or a sibling or, God forbid, a child.

My losses are small ones.

My dog.

Contracts with publishers.

Chances I let slip through my fingers.
My health.
My pride.
My absolutes.
My control.
And even, occasionally, my faith.

Every time I lose something that I wanted to tightly hold, it leaves behind this giant gap. A hole that I quickly try to fill with anything: books, chips and salsa, Netflix, people, running mile after mile, hoping to leave the hurt and loss behind. I have always felt a void. An ache. Like something is missing. And maybe it is because I had youth director after youth director tell me I was created with a God-sized hole that only He can fill. Which led me to believe that if I still feel it, then maybe I don't know God in the right context. That I am doing it wrong. That I don't have enough faith.

I suspect that all that isn't true. That we ache because we were in fact made for more. That we are supposed to long for more, but maybe the kind of more we were made for comes from less. I do not think that the God who formed us from the dust, breathed His very spirit into us and then left this giant hole in our hearts. I doubt He hopes that one day we will ask Him to move in. That right until that moment we've tried to fill the hole with girl-scout cookies or wine or worse, and only after we say the right words that He will slide in and fill us up. He will pull a Jerry McGuire and complete us. Instead, I think He has been there all. Along.

God is not in the gaps.

He has always been about wholeness.

The ache we feel is maybe something we need to shed rather than something we need to fill.

Little by little.

He is like the sculpture. The beautiful part — that was there all along.

All we have to do is remove.

The stuff that gets in the way.

The lies that sometimes are louder than the truth.

The ego. The greed. The grief.

The unnecessary. The excess.

Sometimes we must shed even the good parts that weren't meant to be in our masterpiece.

The beautiful words that are no longer part of our story.

I hate the carving and the pruning.

Losses, even minor ones, seem to flatten me.

Removal is painful.

Good art always is.

He is the potter and I am only the clay.

He is the gardener and I am the vine.

Maybe there is not a God-shaped hole in me. Instead, there is only God.

It is by being made less that we allow the God in us to be revealed.

The love and the beauty and the masterpiece that was in there the whole time.

CONFIRMATION

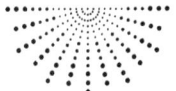

I'VE SPENT DECADES OF MY LIFE TRYING TO BE DIFFERENT from my family, but for a few decades we barely have a choice. Our world is small, and it is all we know, for better or worse. When I was young, I voted the same straight party ticket they did. I cheered for the same teams.

I carried the same faith. Choice, exposure and life experience were limited.

Now, decades later, most of these things have diverged. My world grew. I vote differently. I went to a different college. There are some things I still choose, but there is now a difference between choosing and being chosen for. My choices are mine, for better or worse.

In the Methodist denomination, babies are often baptized and almost teenagers are deemed old enough to decide for themselves. It is then that they can confirm their faith. A faith that was often chosen for them becomes their own to choose. When my son went through confirmation, I was wrapping up graduate school and in a world of pain. Physical pain that I took fistfuls of pills each day to abate. I did not volunteer to help because I pretty much did not volunteer for anything in that stage of my life. It was a blur and a struggle to make it through each day. I was doing my absolute best just to pick him up on time.

I have always wanted to be a person to do big things. I like to think that hard moments would only fortify my relationships, make me stronger and even closer to God. However, when the pills and risky surgery didn't seem to be working, I only felt God's absence. I felt alone. And small. And weak and out of options. And my comforter was not comforting. Hope was terrifying. I had been let down too many times. When things got hard, I didn't suddenly rise to the top. I just mostly went to bed early. And the doctors upped my dose again and again. Even though God felt quiet and I was angry at him, I sought him out over and over again.

I went to church. I read Psalms. I prayed. I asked others to pray for me when I couldn't. I wrote. I tried to be thankful and joyful. It took years, but eventually relief came. Nerves heal slowly. Sometimes miracles happen so gradually that you forget to call them that. I felt stronger, physically, spiritually and mentally.

Four years later, and suddenly it was my daughter's turn for confirmation. My life looked dramatically different, and at what I thought was the tail end of a pandemic, the world looked dramatically different too. My pain, instead of an unwelcome constant companion, had become only an occasional visitor. I had a new job, no graduate school and more free time. After over a year of communal worship not even being an option, I missed church. Despite my daughter's preference, I volunteered to lead a small group for confirmation.

I showed up for the first time in almost a year to the sanctuary. I got to sing and listen to a pastor. (Granted, their primary audience members were barely in middle school). I'm not totally sure I knew what I was getting into, despite the fact that my own sixth grader needed to be bribed with Sonic drinks the first few sessions. When we finally broke out into our small groups, these kids mostly didn't know each other and sat silently when we asked questions. I pulled out my best tools to make them comfortable, and they were still awkward. The masks making all this possible also added to the layer of distance I was trying to close. Once these kids warmed up, they got off topic easily. Any given Sunday, I would have handed over $100 to anyone who volunteered to pray out loud.

I can't blame them. The content is hard.

Why do we believe what we believe and how do we live out our faith?

Damn. I'm still trying to figure that out.

But each week we got in our circles and did our best.

Just a few weeks into confirmation, I realized I had been wrong. About being better. I wasn't. I made an appointment with my neurologist and my therapist. I refilled an old prescription. It all felt like defeat and fear. The pain wasn't so bad yet. My neurologist warned me about the "yet." She told me I needed to take the medicine now to prevent as much damage as possible. That it would do no good to power through; I had to face it and treat it. My counselor asked more about my fear and heart than my physical symptoms. I told her I wasn't sure I could do this all over again. She assumed I meant the pain and the surgery. I did, but I also told her I couldn't face the idea of God being absent again. Maybe that was the biggest fear.

I did not baptize my babies. I wanted to, but my husband, who rarely voices a strong opinion, asked that we wait until it was something they could choose. When I was an infant, a pastor placed a wet hand on my head. A baptism is supposed to be a public profession, and in the case of an infant it is the parents and the congregation professing and promising. Eventually, all these baptized babies will have to confirm for themselves the promises others made on their behalf. At some point in our lives, the faith chosen for us either becomes our own or shapes into something very different.

Despite the return of pain and my personal fear of middle schoolers, I kept volunteering on Sundays. I started to look forward to seeing these kids each week. They started to loosen up, just a little (or occasionally a little too much). Their sarcasm came out, but so did a few thoughtful answers. I did my best to minister, but I was mostly ministered to. Each week, I had to say (and sing) the Apostles' Creed. I had to state what I'd believed in a phase of my life when I needed to be reminded of the promises found there every single week (and honestly every single day).

Once I heard pastor Nadia Bolz-Weber interviewed on NPR, and she talked about the Apostles' Creed in a way I haven't forgotten:

"I don't think faith is given in sufficient quantity to individuals… I think it's given in sufficient quantity to communities." She gave a few examples: Some people think they can't say the Apostles' Creed because they don't believe all that it says. "I'm like, oh, my God. Nobody believes every line of the Creed. But in a room of people…for each line of the Creed, somebody believes it." Faith can (and should) be the work of a community. 7

Yesterday my daughter was confirmed, and the day before that she was baptized in a cold river. I'm not sure what she felt, if she grasped the significance of it, or if she was just hoping to get to pick where we ate dinner. Either way, she chose confirmation in community. That God that is sometimes quiet but has never let me go is the same one she said "yes" to in a crowded sanctuary. Because part of faith in Christ is yes to our own faith but also yes to a community of faith. Though I am well past sixth grade, I felt confirmed as well.

Named. Chosen. A part of a collective and a place where I also say yes.

Nadia's words are a comfort on the days when I am less sure; I'm sure someone in that room will be able to say yes for me.

BITTERSWEET

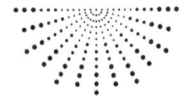

SCROLLING ON SOCIAL MEDIA, I SAW TODAY THAT ONE OF my favorite childhood friends' grandfather passed away. There was a photo of him on the screen. This happens often enough, and most of us (me included) simply scroll past or at best offer our condolences. Yet this photo gave me pause. All at once, I deeply felt the loss of this man I had only met a few times. Whose name I don't even know.

I was five when my own grandfather passed away. He was my only one.

My memories are few and fleeting.

I can't tell you what his voice sounded like or his laugh.

I don't remember if he gave big deep hugs or if he was the kind of guy more likely to offer you a pat on the shoulder. I don't know if he smelled of hair gel or Ivory soap. I don't know if he commanded the room like my father, or if his wife lit up the place instead. Was he harsh or kind or both?

I remember his sagging face. The smell of whiskey. A brown leather couch.

He always had a bag of Hershey's mixed chocolates: plain milk chocolate, Krackle, Mr. Goodbar (the worst pick in the bag) and finally special dark chocolate. He saved the specials for me. He told me I was special. I was so young, but I still ate the bitter chocolate greedily.

For years, I thought I liked it best, but I really only liked the memory.

I liked feeling like the name on the wrapper.

I looked at my friend's grandfather and I did the math. Thirty-nine years since mine had passed away. This is no argument about fairness. My friend lost her father a decade ago and mine still calls me every Sunday, yet I can't help but wonder how it would have felt to have my grandfather longer. To have the same memories and the history that my siblings are old enough to carry.

My friend Laura and I were born only a week or two apart. Our grandfathers were friends. They showed each other pictures and bragged about us. Maybe our friendship began then, with my Paw Paw and her Grandaddy Greening. Two old men (who forty-three years ago weren't nearly as old as I thought they were) bursting with pride over their best girls.

I don't have many memories.

But I carry this picture in my head of my grandfather and hers talking about us.

Loving us in the way only a Paw Paw or a Grandaddy can.

It is a love I barely remember, but it is special.

The memory bittersweet.

My hands started to shake the second I tucked into my pew. I sat where I always sat — on the east side near the back, just like my parents would have done. Everything about the church is familiar, even the carpet, though I don't think I have stepped foot in it in twenty years. There is a good crowd, but I do not recognize a single person. I left my house before 7 a.m. and drove three hours for the funeral of a ninety-year-old man I can barely remember meeting. I certainly would not have recognized him on the street. Nor he me.

The man in the coffin up front is my friend's grandfather. She texted me as she struggled to write his eulogy. I go to watch her honor her grandfather, but I am also there to grieve my own. I don't remember it, but I suspect I went to his funeral thirty-nine years earlier.

It was probably in this exact same room.

Maybe some of the same people were there.

Sitting on these same wooden pews, staring at the burgundy carpet.

The pastor steps up to the lectern to give the sermon and I have to look twice.

My old pastor has returned for the funeral.

The same one I remember from high school.

The same one that confirmed me at twelve and married me and my husband twenty years ago. And from my pew in the back, he looks almost exactly the same, except for his thinning hair. His voice rings with the same inflection and sincerity.

The pastor speaks slowly, simply and with great heart.

I wonder about my childhood faith in this place. In this old and dying church.

About how much I got wrong.

The church itself is slightly smaller than I remember. Like most things from our youth.

And I wonder if this traditional place could hold my now unruly faith.

If there would be room for it here.

The sanctuary is long and narrow.

These days my faith is wide and stretched thin.

But as he speaks, he is so earnest, and I can't help but think maybe it is just true. Then and now. His words are not messy or complicated or political or outdated.

They are simple and heartfelt.
The gospel of John spoken for a man named John.
Spoken for me.
Time plays tricks and does not stand still in a place like this.
It moves backwards and forwards.

A place with so much history houses who we were and maybe even who we will be.

Jesus is the same yesterday today and forever$_8$. And I wonder how much of me is the same.

Most days, I'd like to think I've grown and changed, and my sixteen-year-old me would barely recognize the forty-six-year-old version.

But today, in this familiar pew, I am feeling a little more generous.

I feel like she would, and she'd be glad for the parts she held as well as the ones she outgrew.

Two days later, Ash Wednesday, I stop by my own church on the way to work.

I hesitantly walk into the chapel and stand there while a pastor dips his thumb into the ashes and paints a cross on my forehead. I do not leave it on my head for long, but the scent of the ashes lingers with me all day. I smell of fire and death. It is a reminder that sometimes we need to burn it all down to begin again. What do I need to burn? Control. Expectations. Striving. Unforgiveness.

But maybe the better question is — and a question I felt on those familiar wooden pews:

What do I need to keep?

DUST AND ASHES

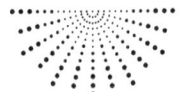

I LEARNED TO DRIVE ON DIRT ROADS, LONG BEFORE I WAS old enough. Long before my feet even reached the pedals. I let my own kids do the same. Find their way on a country gravel road or two ruts in a pasture. Last year, before my daughter had her permit, we let her practice on the dirt roads on vacation.

In the summer we go to the mountains. The last stretch to wherever we stay is always a patch of dirt or gravel. This year, the house my in-laws rented was even farther up the mountain. It took at least fifteen minutes climbing slowly on washboard roads. At some point, my husband even switched gears. The driving is slow, the tires often slipping. Our back windshield was completely covered in dirt and dust. It is harder to drive on the dirt than the pavement, but it somehow seems a safer place to learn. Despite the dust, I can't help but roll my window down and turn up the radio. We have since made the long trek home, all but the first part paved. And still, my husband's car is covered in a fine layer of brown. We may have left the cool of the mountains for our hot Texas summer, but some of the mountains came home with us.

You'd think that over 600 miles, at 75 miles per hour (or maybe a little bit more) would manage to blow all the dust off, but it remains. Turns out dust sticks. There is some science behind it, mostly that static electricity makes dust adhere to surfaces like cars and sandals and bookshelves. There is a literal charge to it. Dust doesn't just settle, it clings.

A few weeks ago, I drove to one of my favorite places. Several of us showed up. All in a very different emotional place from the funeral six months earlier. Then we were buried in our shock and loss and what ifs. The shock of her loss has worn off and life has carried on. Grief now fits like an old pair of shoes. We come back to say goodbye again in a beautiful place full of dust and rocks and rivers. Her cousin read a few words and then stepped forward and spread a handful of ashes. Only this little bit of her remained, and here is exactly where she'd want to be.

When it was my turn, the ashes felt different than I expected. They were coarse, gritty, and heavy in my hand. Closer to a dense sand than leftovers from a campfire. I opened my hand, but only a few blew away. The weight of an entire life remained in my palm. I suppose this is why people say they scatter ashes. You must literally release them. Let them go. Which is a lesson I have recently been learning over and over and over again.

After I let her go, my hand remained covered in a fine layer of dust. I wasn't sure what to do with it. It felt wrong to wipe it on my pants. So, instead, I just left the residue on my hands. The ashes clung to me. My friend, gone now for months, remained. In less physical ways, this place and these people have clung to me for decades, and I'm better for it. Ashes make you let go and cling at the same time. I can't imagine a better picture of my grief or my faith.

I walk the gravel path to my car and make my way down the steep hill.

Past the dorm and the tennis courts and the catwalk.

I wind my way back to the highway.

My car, covered in hill-country dust. Ashes still buried deep in the crevices of my hand.

There is a verse in the Bible where Abraham humbly claims to be "nothing but dust and ashes[9]." Astrophysicist Neil deGrasse Tyson also calls us nothing but dust with a slightly different sentiment: "We are stardust brought to life, then empowered by the universe to figure itself out — and we have only just begun[10]."

On my best days, I am also nothing but dust and ashes.

It is as much an honor as a humbling.

Dusty roads.

Star dust.

Things left behind.

Grief. Love.

Scattered. Clung to.

Maybe the dust and ashes serve as a reminder that the places we leave will always leave their mark on us (or our back windshield).

That the people and places we let go of will cling hard and true to our hearts.

What we carry doesn't have to weigh us down if we are willing to let it go.

I am nothing but dust and ashes.

Just like the dusty roads I learned to drive on, they don't only lead away.

Sometimes they lead us towards.

I am everything, stardust, gravel roads and a handful of ashes.

I have only just begun.

GOOD AND BEAUTIFUL THINGS

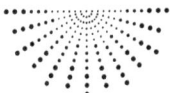

OUR DRIVER PICKS US UP AT THREE IN THE MORNING. THE travel agent assured us that the early wake-up call would be worth it... and the website promised a sky blanketed in soft clouds and a sunrise "bursting forth in a flood of warmth and color."

So I find myself heading up a volcano at a time when I'm usually snoring. Our bus driver warns everyone that it can be cold and windy at the top. I packed a blanket and a sweatshirt and made the mistake of thinking I was prepared.

He tells us that we need to get there early to beat the rush of tourists and claim a front-row seat to the sunrise. *Haleakala* means "House of the Sun" and, according to legend, the demigod Maui set out to lasso the sun in an effort to slow it down. I don't believe in demigods, but I head up over 10,000 feet in the dark to capture the sun myself, and for a glimpse of God's beauty.

We wind our way up the summit...and I'm temporarily glad for the black night so that I cannot see the steep drops. Hours later — still cloaked in darkness — we finally summit. We're told where to stand for the best view and reminded to have our cameras ready. Sunrise is thirty minutes out as we stumble off the bus into the black.

At this altitude, wind whips through my blanket and sleet pelts my face. My friends climb right back on the bus, and I follow them. I was prepared for it to be cool, but not this cold. This is Hawaii, after all. I packed a suitcase full of sundresses, not a winter coat.

I warm under the heater and tell myself that I did not get up at three in the morning to sit on a bus, so I bundle up and venture out again. This time, I walk alone and find only a few people clumped around the crater's edge. My hair flies in my face, the wind blows straight through my layers, and I can't feel my fingers or toes. The crowd is small and there is no need to fight anyone for a good view. Shivering at the lip of the crater for a good twenty minutes, I huddle with strangers who, like me, are waiting for the morning light to streak the sky with color. Eventually, the sky does grow less and less dark — but there is no show. There is no beauty, no sunrise "bursting forth in a flood of warmth and color" to reward me for my early rise, that long drive, or my freezing toes. The sky slowly turns from black to gray with a fog so thick I can barely see a few feet in front of me, much less the island below. My friend finally gets off the bus and comes to find me. She warms my arms gently and tells me, "I think this is it." She sees a weight to my disappointment...that I'm waiting for more than a sunrise.

Somehow, I thought the pain and misery of getting to this volcano would pay off and, after years of my own pain, it's like I need this to be true in my own life. After walking through a difficult season, I need to know that my aches matter. That, despite all that has been heavy and hard, something beautiful is, in fact, on the horizon.

Sometimes God allows hard seasons to draw us towards Him — but sometimes *we* choose to suffer. The two are not always connected. My miserable, sunless sunrise taught me that I had gone too far. I wanted my misery to be rewarded with a holy moment and picture-perfect view. I always want the ache to pay off. I want to push through when I'm not ready. I falsely believe that my faith has to be hard or hurt for it to matter. I want the suffering to bring a reward, but sometimes it only leaves me cold and wet and waiting for something that doesn't turn out how I'd hoped.

Good and beautiful things can come from hard and horrible places, but there is no reason I should think that they have to. I like hard things. I used to love running long distances, accomplishing a challenging task, and persevering through difficult seasons. However, what I'm starting to learn from sunrises, volcanoes, and patient friends is that these things aren't good because they are hard. They are good because God is. Full stop.

Eventually, our driver transports us back to our hotel to rest and dry off. Later, we find a little bit of sun and enjoy our day — a day that started way too early on a bus...but ended on the water with a sunset filled with warmth and color. In Psalm 113:3, I'm reminded that, "From the rising of the sun to the place where it sets, the name of the Lord is to be praised[11]." Pondering this Psalm made me realize that all throughout my day, God was present and worthy of praise — both in the gray sunrise and as the sun slowly dipped behind the bay.

As the sun set, the sky turned fifteen different shades of pink and yellow and orange. It was perfect. No suffering required. All I had to do was open my eyes.

ADVENT AND ORDINARY TIME

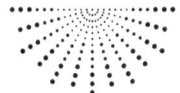

EARLY FEBRUARY - ORDINARY TIME

The church calendar is broken up into three seasons. It begins with Advent, which is a time of preparation for the celebration of Christ's birth. Advent leads us to Christmas and Epiphany. Sometime in spring we begin Lent, a time of remembrance of the love and sacrifice of His death that goes through Easter and Pentecost, but most of the year is spent in what the church creatively named Ordinary Time.

I did some research$_{12}$ and ordinary time is not actually its own distinct season; it is a way to describe the in-between times. The everyday. The flat tire. The broken dishwasher. Coffee with friends. What to cook for dinner. Soccer practice. The church doesn't break up time based on the weather; instead, time is based on new life, death and all the in-between. Preparation, remembering and the rest of the days that might overwise run together.

It is easy to find descriptions of Advent and Lent, but less is written about the in-between, though most of our time is spent living there. According to the greater church, ordinary here does not mean what I think it means. It doesn't mean simple, plain or nothing special; instead, it means that these in-between weeks are numbered. Ordinary is a reference to the idea of ordinal numbers. An ordinal number just lists position (first, second, third, etc.). In other words, the idea of ordinary time means: it is counted. It matters.

All this in-between stuff is important. Advent is to prepare; Lent is to remember; ordinary time, however, is where we are meant to live and grow. The Roman calendar begins in January and ends in December. The church calendar is reversed. Advent is the beginning, but we end with Ordinary Time. We prepare. We grow. We remember. We live. All of it matters.

October - Still Ordinary Time

I am sitting in church. It has been over six weeks since I have sat in these pews. The last time I was here I left in the middle. I said I was running an errand, but more likely I was running away. Suddenly we sing a song. Oceans[13].

"Where feet may fail and fear surrounds me
You've never failed and You won't start now
Standing and trusting."

My chin starts to quiver. I try to hide behind my coffee cup and wipe away the few tears that slip out anyway. I love this song, but I cannot sing it this morning. I am so mad at myself for not being able to do this. For being angry. For feeling sorry for myself. The sermon is on how heavy our burden is and how focusing on the right things will lift it off. The pastor at the front tells us to imagine a heavy weight on us, and then suddenly it being lifted.

I think this is bullshit.

I do not have to imagine a heavy weight. It is there. It is back. It has slammed me into the ground again. I am afraid to imagine it being lifted because the memory of the lightness is too hard, making the weight only seems heavier.

I am angry at the cheapness of his words. How easy he makes it sound. And that, again, I must not be doing or saying or believing the right things. In this moment I can promise that I am not. I feel like maybe my faith has been cheap and shallow if it is this easily rattled.

I tell a few people how I feel. The pain that has returned and the emptiness that hope seems to have left behind in its flight. The neurologist gets me in that day (this is a small miracle.) He says he is so sorry. He increases my dosage and tells me to come back in a few months. I go home emptied out. Drained of hope and trying to formulate some idea of what to do, and mostly only come up with things not to do.

A friend asks me how Jesus and I are in this season. I answer honestly, if Jesus was my friend on social media, I think I might have unfriended him. Or at least hidden Him for a little while. It is not that I don't know that He is good and true, I do. I just don't feel it in this moment. If this is his plan, then it is a shitty plan. I feel whiny; I recognize that I am not dying. My family is amazing. I take a page from Ann Voskamp[14] and start listing the good. I look for beautiful around me — I find it and I snap pictures of the moon and write lists of the things I am glad for. I keep another running list in my head of all the things that could be worse. Yet thankfulness and perspective are not always the magical cures we want them to be.

Prayer, like everything these days, comes hard. I read about big wild prayers and think that maybe I should be praying wilder. Or more often. Or more faithfully. Or fasting. More of anything that will get me a response. My prayers feel empty and repetitive and selfish but most days I still mumble them even if they are seeded with doubt.

I have not gone to God last.

I have prayed wildly and nakedly and broken.

I have asked to be healed, for relief, for comfort.

I have asked to be able to trust again.

I keep asking.

Hope, I suppose, keeps asking even when she doesn't trust the answers or sing out loud.

December - Advent

Usually, people think of Advent as a season of waiting, but I like how Sarah Bessey puts it: as a "season of living in the tension[15]." It is both the time of anticipatory joy and of longing. The joy of Christmas and still a longing for all things to be made right. One of my favorite Christmas hymns has this well-worn line, "A thrill of hope the weary world rejoices[16]". We are weary and we rejoice. Advent gives us permission to do both, which is good because I can't think of a season where my calendar is fuller.

During Advent we light candles in the same order each week, counting our way down. First is hope, then peace, then joy and finally love. We need hope and peace to speak to our weary hearts before we are ready for the joy. Recently I have started to understand the waiting. I thought I knew. Waiting in lines so deep at Target they are wrapped around the cosmetic counter. Waiting for the bell to ring. Waiting for acceptance letters and medical results, but I didn't know.

Waiting and longing for what you know will happen doesn't seem to count; that is just marking time. Waiting when you don't know. When you aren't sure. Hoping when there is nothing else to do. Those are lessons I have learned the hard way. Back in Ordinary Time, I was desperate and empty. Now I feel less of that. More hopeful. More peaceful. Making my way towards joyful.

I wasn't sure where faith and trust fit into Advent until I read Sarah Bessey's continuation on the longing of Advent and moving into joy. "So I didn't learn to practice joy until I learned to practice grief, and I didn't learn how to do either one of those things well until I learned that God can be trusted[15]."

Trusted to show up to a tired and scared teenage girl over two thousand years ago.

Trusted to show up to a tired and scared mother today.

Every night during this season in my house, we light a candle and let just a little of it burn down. The days are marked. The wax melts.

The candle burns down and some of the edges and the pain and the hard seems to melt down as well. The songs get easier to sing. The pain has eased. The silence is less loud.

The darkness is filled with candlelight. With hope. With peace. With joy.

MARCH – Holy Thursday

This morning, I left my house twenty minutes earlier than usual. I pulled into my church parking lot before driving to work. The lot was almost empty, but I had read in my bulletin last week that the chapel would be open from 6-8 a.m. for anyone who wanted to take communion on this Holy Thursday.

I love the act of communion and have been getting up early every day this week to observe Holy Week. I thought that this morning, instead of sitting on my couch reading and quiet, maybe I should go to the chapel. After I pulled in, I immediately thought about turning around and getting a coffee. I was a little uncomfortable about the idea of showing up at church at 6:27 a.m. And I didn't know what to expect. If this would be weird. If I was supposed to say anything or do anything special that I didn't know about. I know this place and space, but occasionally I found myself wondering about the rules or expectations. Church makes sense on Sunday mornings or weeknight Bible studies, but on a quiet Thursday I wasn't so sure.

I worried about who would be there. If there would be a lot of people, businessmen off to work, those religious types doing some serious prayer or a bunch of old ladies who couldn't sleep. I even doubted if I had the right day. I could still just go to Starbucks. I had to keep telling myself to get over the awkward and just go inside.

I walked into the chapel, which was totally empty except for a minister in a robe reading in the front pew. She welcomed me and told me to kneel at the altar. Just me. And she read aloud a passage from Luke.

For just me.

And she offered me the body and the blood. Shed for me. And in this moment, it was only me.

Church is so often collective that I forget our faith is also individual. It took an empty chapel for the realization of what Christ did for me, just me, to land. This moment alone, and not a church filled with people. Or believers all over the world, but just me. Shook me in my soul. And I lingered at the altar a bit. And the pastor returned to her pew and continued her reading. And I walked out to my car and wept for what Christ did for me.

Just me.

And just for you.

EASTER 2020

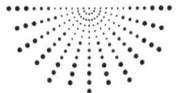

My family usually sat in the same place. A hard wooden pew near the back on the left-hand side. My mom insisted I wear a dress, wrangle myself into pantyhose and wear nice shoes (not Keds). We would go to Sunday school. The kids would wait in hallways for our parents' class to end. Hoping that there would be donuts leftover. More often than not, we skipped "big church," visited family and picked up fried chicken on our way home. Church was pews, pipe organs, air hockey in the youth building, polite conversations and boxes of chicken.

At summer camp, church was at the top of what felt like the highest hill in Hill Country.

We sat on dusty stone benches in our sweaty Sunday whites. Someone strummed a guitar, and we all sang along. Church was aching legs, BBQ down by the river and clumsy chords.

In college I made it to church on Sundays about half the time. Occasionally hungover. Always tired. I would still find a dress but had long ditched the pantyhose. We shopped around, yet my favorite Sunday church was in an old BBQ restaurant. The old dance floor transformed into a pulpit. Church was still dresses and folding chairs, often followed by cheap tacos.

Real church in college happened on Thursday nights in a basement of the Wesley Foundation with watered-down Kool-Aid and day-old donated donuts.

We struggled to find a church after we got married but eventually landed in one twenty minutes away. Too big, too fancy and too conservative, but it came with the perfect group of friends for us at the time. Eventually, we moved to another. And then another. To one that felt more like the ones from home. Back to hard pews and stained glass. Sundays and eventually Saturdays.

I go as I am, but usually, at least take a shower first. My kids ask if we are eating with friends after, because we usually are. I occasionally serve the bread and wine, but more often I help with the small row of youth that show up on a Saturday night. I have been here for years. Sometimes in the chapel. Sometimes in the loft, but these days in the sanctuary. I have felt nothing, and I have also felt full. I have longed for and looked for. I have been emptied out and filled up. I have doubted. I have sung loud and off-key. I have mouthed the words. I haven't even bothered. I have listened closely. And I have written to-do lists in the bulletin.

Church is wooden pews. Familiar songs and faces. Teens sharing about their week. Jeans and t-shirts. Full tables. Broken bread and grape juice and an honest heart.

Today as I walk around my neighborhood for the third time, I long for a sanctuary.

Stained glass and guitars. And I feel all the things I have grown used to inside a church: doubt and fire and fullness and emptiness. I miss the feel of a hard pew or folding chair. I even miss the scratch of pantyhose.

Tomorrow I will sit on my couch and watch church on my computer screen. And I will say "He is risen" while wearing yoga pants. Later I will Zoom with my family.

No Easter brunch. No flowers tucked into crosses. No lilies lining the altar.

My heart will ache, but I expect it to also to be warmed, because my God has never been pinned down to pews and steeples.

There was no church on the first Easter. Only friends gathered and grieving. Full of loss and uncertainty, which sounds awfully familiar. And a few women who ventured out to find an empty tomb. Christ's first words to them, "Do not be afraid" are words I still need to hear. Church will be my couch, fuzzy socks and all the schoolwork pushed aside to make room for a meal. Church will be a longing for each other. Church will be worshiping alone. Together.

And I will find sanctuary in my living room.

Holiness on my couch.

Pantyhose completely optional.

TURNING THE QUESTION

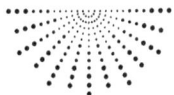

I TAUGHT HIGH SCHOOL CHEMISTRY AND PHYSICS FOR almost two decades. Most people grimace when you mention stoichiometry, kinematics, or cellular respiration. However, the struggle is rarely with the content, but usually with thinking patterns. Given enough practice, I could teach almost anyone how to balance an equation, yet the harder lesson was always teaching a sixteen-year-old to ask good scientific questions and how to work through them. They mostly just ask to go to the bathroom, for extra credit or what will be on the test.

When children are young, they ask questions incessantly, but by the time they became teenagers, many of my students stopped asking out of curiosity and understanding and instead asked only from compliance.

One of the core practices of science education is inquiry. Teaching through inquiry requires an investigative approach to teaching and learning where students are provided with opportunities to explore a problem, search for possible solutions, make observations, ask questions, test out ideas, and think creatively. In summary, more questions and less answers. More doing and less memorizing. This practice is supported by almost every educational entity; however, it is not always embraced. I suspect this is because inquiry sounds great in theory but is much harder to pull off effectively.

Sure, there are limitations with supplies, pacing calendars and standardized tests. However, the main reason teachers don't always embrace inquiry, at least for me, is because it is hard to let go of control. Discovery takes more time. It isn't a straight line. You can't be certain where a student will land, even if the data promises the learning will be more impactful. If we are so afraid to do this in science class, where questions are not only permitted but required, it is no wonder we often struggle to do this in places of faith. Discovery takes more time. It isn't a straight line. You can't be certain where someone will end up.

It would be easy for me to forget or minimize the struggle in giving up control and allowing people to wrestle with a question long enough to find their own answer, except for the fact that I've also parented toddlers. Toddlers constantly insist on doing it themselves. Letting them do this ensures frustration, because I can do whatever "it" is so much faster. Thankfully, I let my own toddlers struggle, or else I'd still be tying my son's shoes or doing my daughter's laundry. I have three degrees in education, but it still floors me to realize that we learn more from questions and struggle than from answers.

Inquiry isn't just for science class; it is the beauty of a good mystery novel or crime show. No one wants to read a book or watch a show that is too obvious or with a twist too obscure. The satisfaction lies in our efforts to figure it out, not to just watch the story unfold from the sidelines. Inquiry explains why I watch *Only Murders in the Building*, listen to Crime Junkies, or pick up the next Louise Penny novel. In an article by the BBC on why people are so obsessed with true crime shows, the BBC informs[17] us that our fixation on these shows is less about the criminal misdemeanor and more about our nature. "We instinctively want to discover the 'who', 'what', 'when' and 'where'". Our brains are hard wired to discover and ask questions. Good writing (be it a TV show, podcast, or mystery novel) allows us to figure it out rather than to simply be told. Inquiry invites us into the story as a participant rather than just a spectator. Russian playwright Anton Chekov gave us four classics, and also this quote: "The role of the artist is to ask questions, not answer them.[18]" Inquiry is a best practice not only in science, but also in art.

I think Jesus might have sided with Anton Chekov. In the gospels, Jesus asks at least 307 questions. He is asked 187 but only directly answers a few. Jesus knew something about teaching, maybe that is why Mary called him Rabonni (great teacher). What if faith, like education, was more about questions than answers? More about figuring it out and struggling rather than perfect performance? What if healing is found mostly in exploring the questions rather than seeking answers? What if learning is more about asking the right questions rather than bubbling in the right circles? What if why matters so much less than how or the next right step?

One problem with inquiry is that older students have forgotten how to ask good questions. Adults are even worse. When my own kids were young, they constantly bombarded me with whys all day long.

Why are owls nocturnal?

Why do I have to take a shower?

Why does that cloud look like a bear with a tutu on?

Why does gum stick?

Why is twelveteen not a number?

Eventually, after years of hearing moms and teachers and everyone else responding with answers like "Later", "Because" and "I don't know", those "why" questions stop flowing. By the time my students hit high school, I had to pry scientific questions out of them and bribe them with candy, stickers, or bonus points. Even then, most didn't ask very good questions. Their questions still sounded a lot like my five-year-old asking why.

Why questions are really hard to answer.

I can tell you how neurons fire. But not why. I can calculate the speed of light. But not tell you why things get all crazy when you start moving that fast. I can tell you how far away the moon is. But not why it ended up there. I can observe altruistic behaviors in animals but not tell you why they protect each other. At least not with certainty.

Why questions are hard to calculate, observe and measure.

A decade ago, I attended some training put out through the Smithsonian Institute, and they taught us how to "turn the question." Turning the question means taking a why question, pulling out variables and finding something students can do or investigate. For example, if someone asks, "Why does water boil?" — that is a tough question to investigate. However, students could test at what temperature water boils, if hot water boils faster than cold water, if different liquids boil at different temperatures, if adding something to the water makes it boil faster, and so on.

Turning the questions helps get you unstuck. Pretty much the trick and thing the instructor stated, which I dutifully jotted down in my lesson plan book and still remember a decade later, was this:

"How can the question be turned into a practical action or something useful?"

I am a girl coming out of a long season of questions and especially whys. Most of which have nothing to do with science, but lie more on the lines of my faith and my heart. The whys weren't really getting me anywhere, except for more questions. I took a page from my lesson plan and wondered how I could use inquiry on my heart. I attempted to turn those hard questions into things I could explore or looked for places to apply practical actions. I leaned into curiosity and found that just like in the classroom (and with toddlers), turning questions can be more frustrating, and certainly takes longer, but it makes a much bigger impact.

Several years ago, I had brain surgery to cure a chronic pain condition. I have trigeminal neuralgia, which at the time sent painful electric shocks through my skull hundreds of times a day. The pain was bad enough for me to let a surgeon cut a hole in my head in an attempt to find relief.

Surgery was supposed to heal me, but in the immediate year that followed it, the pain got worse instead of better. I tried literally everything to lessen my pain. I visited neurologists, chiropractors, pastors, and an acupuncturist. Eventually, I decided if I couldn't fix the outside of my brain, then maybe I could fix the inside. Chronic pain pushed me to ask dozens of impossible questions. A few started with why, but I also wanted to know how to move forward. I thought maybe a therapist would be able to answer my questions for me. I could not have been more wrong. She did not give me answers. Instead, she gave me a hundred more questions. She gave me space week after week to ask them and struggle through them. Of course, the questions came with tools and strategies that made sitting in them so much easier. Which is good, because the questions keep getting harder.

The questions and not the answers have helped me heal. Eventually my pain eased. Healing and discovery take time. They aren't a straight line. The answers weren't the answer; instead, I've found the answer is often the question and curiosity.

Each time I find myself stuck, it is usually because I'm looking for answers instead of questions. Or I'm simply asking the wrong ones. When I can't get past the why questions, I'm learning to stay curious, to turn my own questions and ask, what is the next right thing I can do from here?

Jesus was a master of turning the question but in a different way. When people asked him questions, he often answered with another question. (I'm sure his friends swore under their breath each time he did this.) For example, in Matthew $_{19}$ when his disciples asked where they could get enough bread, he responded by asking them, "How many loaves do YOU have?" He gave them the next right thing and an opportunity. He asked hundreds of questions, but he only asked one three times[20].

Do you love me?

Jesus knew the answer to this, but he still asked it, not once but thrice. Sometimes questions are an invitation to find our own answers. To know. To make amends. The answer was of course, yes, even after Peter had really screwed it up. Sometimes I wonder why a kind and gentle Jesus didn't just tell Peter that all was forgiven. Surely Jesus understood that Peter and the disciples were scared and afraid and grieving. He could have simply given him a vision for the man he wanted Peter to be. Just promise Peter that he is a rock. But first Jesus presses, and turns the question on Peter. He asks. Jesus did not need the assurance, but Peter did. And he knew he wouldn't be physically present for long, and he needed Peter to really believe it. That kind of knowing doesn't come from telling, it comes from asking. Over and over and over.

Sometimes I know the right answers, but I don't know how to feel them. Maybe there is something to answering the same questions over and over and over again. To inquiring. To struggling. To finding the answers for ourselves.

Yes. Yes. Yes.

PART II
RECKLESS HOPE

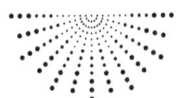

"Hope, like every virtue, is a choice that becomes a practice that becomes spiritual muscle memory. It's a renewable resource for moving through life as it is, not as we wish it to be."—— **Krista Tippett**

THE NOT NOTHING

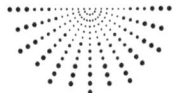

I HAVE A COMPLICATED RELATIONSHIP WITH HOPE. HOPE can break your heart. It has broken mine. I have lived through seasons where hope was all I had, but also seasons where hope felt dangerous, reckless even. When nothing seemed to be working, while I had tried all the next steps. Where the miracle didn't seem like it was coming.

How do you hold on to hope in those moments when you can't face another disappointment? Hope can be the most reckless thing of all. Love is sometimes blind, but hope knows the heartache and chooses it again anyway.

Recently I lost a friend in the most tragic way. My beautiful friend took a gun and a bottle of pills and drove to a park while her family was at church. I'd been worried about her, but I had never imagined this. She parked in a parking space, facing a busy street, only slightly obscured by a row of bushes. I'm not sure how long she sat there. If she hesitated. If she cried or prayed or felt like she was performing some kind of mercy. All I know is that some time, while her family sat in a pew across town, she sent a few texts that never went through before turning the gun on herself.

We looked for her for days.

And there she was right there the whole time.

I found her eventually. Thankfully, the police had found her first.

But I still couldn't drive home.

I don't remember most of that week.

I remember voice after voice breaking on the phone. Question after question.

I remember trying to work and staring for hours at my computer screen.

I remember sobbing on the floor of my laundry room.

I remember dry heaving in driveways and church parking lots.

I remember ordering a dress to wear to her funeral.

I remember grabbing the hand next to me.

I remember my own hand shaking as I spoke. Not from nerves but from an ache.

I remember telling her aunt that first night that I didn't want to go to sleep.

Because at least when she was missing, I could hope that she was alive somewhere.

And going to sleep would mean waking up in a world where I knew she was gone forever.

Going to sleep meant letting go of that hope.

But it was already gone.

She was already gone.

But hope is funny. It can run out and show up again, just when you think all has been lost. And maybe that is why Hebrews$_{21}$ tells us to hold on to it. Hold on to hope. Grasp tightly to the last thread. Or the thread after that. Or just the hand next to you.

In those days, I had friends reeling from the same loss. Several have let go of their faith. Or maybe it let go of them. Maybe it is too big of an ask sometimes- to believe in something so messy and complicated and disappointing. A God who lets friends get so empty they leave a wake and two daughters behind. I don't try to shove my faith on them because I hardly understand it myself, but I don't blame others looking for comfort anywhere they can find it. In tattoos and butterflies and silver linings that I can't quite find yet. I also don't know how to not believe. I wonder if that is enough. To believe in something because you are so afraid of nothing.

I have intended to go there. To park in the same spot and tell my friend what I wish I could have told her that day. I want to tell her that she isn't alone. That she is loved. That it gets better. To hold on to her long enough to send the right texts or drive her car back home.

I'm hoping it will make me feel better, somehow pardon me for my own failures here.

I want a closure. A stitching up of this place where my heart has been ripped open.

I want it to make sense.

I don't know what I think will happen.

That I will feel something. That I will hear God or my friend or both.

I don't do it for weeks.

I know there are ashes somewhere waiting. Tucked in a closet or a drawer.

Just a handful. I don't ever ask about them. I avoid driving past this park. My body always alerting me when I get close.

This morning, I am empty. I am sad and feel alone and angry. I feel helpless, I suppose like she did, and I get this small voice in my head that tells me to go. That now is the time, and I think surely it is a mistake. Today I am not strong enough. I feel less certain of all the things I had wanted to say. That I don't carry hope or certainty. That I feel too alone to go to this lonely place. That I don't know how to speak hope to a ghost. That I don't have any to share.

I'm supposed to pick up her girls in a few hours, and I'm not sure I can do it.

Over the years I've learned to listen to this voice, and so I go. My hands shake and my eyes spill over their lids before I slide into the parking space. I see that day. Police tape, doors open, cameras taking photo after photo and phones ringing. The past is playing out in my present, but I start talking anyways.

I talk to my lost friend.

I tell her she isn't alone.

I don't feel anything. I don't feel God or hope or her.

Part of me understands and the rest is angry.

I give up my certainty and my pep talk and my absolve.

Instead, I tell her that I don't know what to do either.

That I need her help.

I don't know if I'm talking to my friend or my God anymore, and I suppose it doesn't matter.

I tell her I need to know what to do with her girls and her friends in this wake. That everything feels like it has fallen apart.

That I need her fire and her certainty and boldness.

Even though I suppose she let go of all that too.

I don't make any promises, because I know how it feels to have them broken.

I tell her I'm sorry. I tell her I'm afraid. I swear at her for leaving us all here.

I hate her and love her, and because I came here so empty, a tiny bit of me can understand. I ask for help again and again. I wish she had. I wish I knew how to do it better. But eventually my eyes stop flooding. My heart settles just a little. My hands steady.

I talk to her like she is there and if I try hard enough for me almost to see her. But mostly I don't.

I don't feel better, but I don't feel worse either.

I feel slightly unburdened.

I feel like maybe this isn't where I find absolution, but instead where I find permission to speak freely. This space isn't holy or haunted, yet it is at least honest.

I go home and shower. I wash the red from my eyes.

I pick up her girls. They are her.

The oldest quiet but determined. No nonsense. More grown than she should be.

The uncertainty my friend always covered up, laid bare in her thirteen-year-old body.

The youngest, loud and fiery and forever critical, attention-seeking and unsatisfied.

Like their mom, they are hard, but easy to love.

The anger in me quiets to a subtle seethe.

It should be uncomfortable and forced, but they argue and giggle and eat everything in sight.

They are ravenous.

I want hope to be certain and steady and solid. I want it to be a fire and a force.

I want an unwavering promise.

But instead it is just a maybe.

A quiet thud on a monitor.

It is putting your car in reverse.

It is trying again.

It is asking for help even when you don't get it the first time.

Hope is the most courageous thing I can name.

It says, maybe it gets better. Maybe it will be different. Maybe it is worth the pain.

Maybe all this matters.

Maybe the story isn't over yet.

And here is the hardest truth:

Hope will still disappoint.

Hope isn't what I wanted it to be.

It is a faint flicker instead of a bright light.

Hope is not certain. It wavers and questions.

But it is the one thing you can cling to when there is nothing else.

Hope is the not nothing.

Sometimes it is the only thing.

Hope is not the silver lining, but the seed watered from our despair.

Hope is living in this terrible world and still finding the parts that are beautiful.

And I'm ravenous for it.

FLOORBOARDS

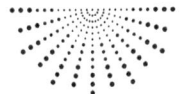

MODELS OF THE BRAIN LINE THE COUNTER AS AN assistant takes my blood pressure, which spikes way too high. Today my blood pressure is the least of my problems. I swear I see sympathy on the nurse's face before she sends the surgeon back.

Dr. Bianca commands the tiny patient room and begins talking immediately in a thick Italian accent. He explains the procedure in great detail. He speaks slowly and instructively though I will be asleep the whole time. I want to make a joke that this isn't brain surgery, except in this case it is exactly brain surgery. He shares percentages, risks and possible complications. He shows me my MRI, and I cannot look him in the eye. I stare compulsively at his hands. His nails, short and clean, his fingers, bare and slender. I can barely take in his words but can tell you he has a small scar just under the knuckle on his right thumb and that his index finger is almost even in length to his middle one. I pray that these hands are sure and steady.

I cry again in the parking garage, mostly from the intensity of my last hour but also because I have no idea where I had parked my car. A different person entirely parked it. The me who had not just agreed to have a one-inch hole drilled into her head. I cry and wonder if I am just being dramatic. I do not have a tumor or a brain bleed or anything else that would require medical intervention, but I have spent the last several years in unbearable nerve pain. Many days I cannot parent or do my job or talk. I have a condition that is sometimes called the suicide disease. I wish I could tell you that I don't know why.

I've read a tale about a farmer and his dog in pain that hit home for me[22]. The farmer spends most of his days sitting on the porch, hanging out with his dog. A friend walks past and approaches. Before his friend can say hello, the dog yelps and squeals and sounds miserable in every way. "What's the matter with your dog?" asks the friend. "He's lying on a nail that's poking up from the floorboards," the farmer responds. "Why doesn't he just get up?" asks the friend. The farmer pauses and wisely replies, "Don't hurt enough yet."

It took me years, but when I finally asked my neurologist for a referral to a neurosurgeon, he responded with, "I wondered how long it would take you to ask." Doctors, needles and hospitals scare me. I fear breathing tubes, titanium plates and the dozen things that can go wrong but probably won't. The surgeon told me that he had an 85% success rate and that he's only lost one person on the table. I'm afraid of that 15% and especially afraid of a second loss. I have young kids, a husband and a hundred reasons to not have optional brain surgery. But each day I take fistfuls of pills that make me get drowsy and forget words. I live in constant pain. Electric shocks jolt through my brain and down my face when I talk, eat, or kiss my own kids goodnight. The wind causes an attack, keeping me from enjoying a good patio or cheering on my kids from the sidelines of their soccer games. A blanket brushes my face in my sleep, and I wake up screaming. In other words, it hurts enough to try and get up off the floorboards.

The day before surgery, I hand the valet my keys. This feels symbolic; after tomorrow I won't be able to drive for over a month. My keys are my first submission. Next, I give up my savings. I sign a bill for enough money to take my family to Disney World, possibly twice. A volunteer escorts me straight to radiology, and I find no comfort in the room labeled "Autopsy" directly across the hall. I count breaths through another MRI, followed by a CT scan, followed by a chest X-ray, followed by a urine test, blood work and an EKG. Eventually, I end up in a private office with a nurse whose job requires her to take more blood and tell me what I need to know for the next day. She takes my temperature, my weight and my blood pressure (which is still too high). I sign form after form ensuring no liability if I land in the 15% or don't even make it off the table. She carefully goes over everything I need to do in the next twenty-four hours: washing with the sterile soap, what meds to take, when to stop eating and how much hair they are likely to shave.

I have had surgery before, so this isn't my first pre-op rodeo, but then she takes a new turn. She reminds me to bring a will, a living will and power of attorney to the hospital. I only have the first and call a lawyer friend who shows up to my home later that night. We find a witness to watch me sign the required forms in my shaky hand. Apparently, there is a lot to do before getting up off the floorboards, dozens of submissions and a notary.

Eventually the nurse finishes and gives me the floor for questions. I have dozens.

"How long will the procedure take?"
"Who will talk to my husband?"
"How long will I be on a ventilator?"
"How long do I stay in ICU?"
"When will I wake up?"
"When will I be able to talk?"
"When will my family be able to see me?"
"How bad will it hurt?"
"It depends," she responds to almost every one of them.

By this point, my eyes are about to spill over, and I desperately want her to ignore this fact. To pretend I'm not on the edge. Instead, she looks me in the eye, hard. She asks if I have kids, and I can only nod.

"Ten and six," I eventually stammer while looking at the floor.

"Me too. And a three-year-old. Don't let them see you in ICU," she advises, "They will allow it, but don't do it."

"I have no intention of having either of them within a two-hundred-mile radius of ICU," I assure her.

I try to laugh, to banter, to make this casual and nothing. She keeps looking me in the eye. I keep staring at the floor. I appreciate her kindness. I really do. I just don't want it. I don't want this kind nurse to see all my fear. To see me so exposed and seen through, even more than all the thousands of dollars' worth of imaging I just sat through. I don't want her or anyone else to try and make me feel better. I don't want to be in this hard plastic chair with a hospital band on my wrist, my arms bandaged and one vein already completely blown. I want to be at the pool, or beach, or even just on my couch. The dentist. The gynecologist. Walmart. Anywhere. Else.

Except maybe on a porch with a nail poking up.

I MET a friend for dinner a few weeks before my surgery whom I had not seen for a while. She wanted all the details and my assurance that my decision to have a risky surgery was not drastic. She wanted to make certain that I had weighed all my options. I told her that everyone has their share of pain management. Maybe theirs is physical, like mine, or maybe it is grief or depression or loss or unmet hopes. I told her I have spent the last few years avoiding things that I love, just not to trigger it or make it worse. The pain was still there, even when I did everything I could to avoid it. I told her sometimes we can do the harder, scarier thing to try and fix the root. This was never easy, always invasive and never without risks. Whatever kind of pain we carry. We can avoid, manage and lie in it. We can mask the ache or we can get up. Writing advice that I have heard at least a dozen times, "Write from the scar, not the wound." Now I write from both.

Today, years later, I have a four-inch scar that snakes just behind my left ear. The pain subsided but did not disappear. Surgery helped but did not cure.

I got up. I keep getting up. That is its own relief.

CEILING FANS

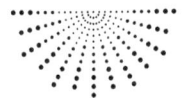

THIS BED IS GETTING OLD, BUT MY HEAD IS STILL pounding. Medicine bottles line the bookcase with a journal of when I took which pill so I don't get confused. I can't remember the last time I put on pants with a zipper. I'm pretty sure that this is a sneak peak of my life in forty years.

I am not sure if it is the teacher in me or just my temperament, but I look at situations and try to figure out what I am supposed to learn from it. Because I think that surely things have a purpose. Although I think the verse has it the other way around.

"A time for every purpose.[23]"

Not a purpose for every time.

So maybe it isn't my job to find it, but that doesn't keep me from trying.

THE LAST FEW weeks are a fog that I am slowly coming out of. A fog of headaches. Naps. Walks with wobbly legs. Worry. Prayer. Homework. And the doorbell ringing with food, groceries, flowers or just a friendly face. Once I had a friend who thought it would be a good idea if we shared with each other the three biggest things we did poorly. (For the record, this is a terrible idea.) The last thing on my list was receiving. It is something I haven't really gotten better at in the last fifteen years. I'm sure like most of my sins, its root is tangled with pride and a sense of worth. But most days I open the door and receive because I have no other choice.

With receiving comes overwhelming gratitude. For this provision, for this manna. That shows up over and over and over again. And I think, this is what I am learning as a firsthand witness to the body of Christ serving me. It is hard to wrap my scarred throbbing head around it. By itself that would be enough, but it is not the only thing. I have also learned a desperate hope.

Optional brain surgery is no easy thing, and I don't just mean for me. There are living wills and powers of attorney to be signed. Large checks to be written, and family and friends who have rearranged entire weeks just to help or sit by you in the hospital. You want it to be worth it. To tell them this pain and expense and fear and inconvenience were for something. To smile big and promising through the morphine. However, that is not exactly how things panned out. They say on the internet, which is the last place anyone who is sick should be spending much time, that you know immediately if the surgery worked. That the pain is gone. Or it isn't, and maybe try again later.

I woke up about five hours later. There was oxygen up my nose, and I had a sore throat from the breathing tube that had been down my throat. My head felt heavy, like I couldn't move it. But when I smiled, I did not get shocked. I kissed my husband and I brushed my teeth. Both those things had been excruciating before and now nothing. My husband profusely thanked the doctor. My first night in ICU was rough. No one warned me about the swelling, but the worst thing was about twenty-four hours later when I felt the tiniest of twinges. I switched pain meds. I tried to be as still as possible. I barely ate. I barely talked for days. The shocks still came, more and more frequently.

Eventually, after proving to nurses and physical therapists that I could walk, breathe and remember who the president was, I was pushed in a wheelchair to the exit. I got in the car, possibly more afraid than I had gotten out of it four days before. I lay in bed. My head pounding. Trying to be still and quiet. I downloaded a counting app and hit the button on my phone every time I got shocked. The shocks were not as long or painful as before, but I gave up when I got to a 100 that first day. My heart sank. I took my pain pills and prayed. I desperately asked for this to go away. I wondered what else I could do or try (acupuncture, essential oils, Botox, a weird diet) or what things I needed to give up (coffee, wine, running, talking).

I wondered if this was it. If this was my future. Pain, with very few options. Pain that would probably get worse. I'd read online about people who had this procedure up to four times, seeking relief, and I just couldn't imagine doing it again. Ever.

I prayed feverishly before going to bed. And when I woke up, and every time, my nerves reminded me. In desperation hoping and praying to be healed. Suddenly, I recognized the desperate hope that I know some of my own friends have felt. In the midst of crisis. Of infertility. Of cancer. Of prayers that seemed to go unanswered. I knew enough to catch myself trying to bargain with God. That He was not that kind of God. I knew enough to think that maybe I should need more faith or more Joel Osteen quotes. That He was not that God either. Frustrated. Defeated. I prayed. And slept. And took sleeping pills and avoided people asking questions about how I felt or if it had worked.

Things were so much better than they had been, but I was so deeply disappointed. And I did not want to see that disappointment reflected on anyone else's face. Desperately hopeful, I kept praying. Because that is pretty much all you can do when you are flat on your back. But I also tried to figure out where to go from there. How long to sulk. How I didn't deserve to. That my family did so much for this. That I can't do it again. Not the money. Or the time. Or the fear. I remember wanting to take pain medicine just to sleep. Not to think. Not to deal with the disappointment, because that was so much harder to endure than pain. I rationed the pain pills out slowly instead. I remember lying there thinking...*this is the rest of my life*. That this was the hand I have been dealt. And at the time it seemed like a shitty hand. But plenty of people get dealt bad hands. Plenty worse than mine. Forgive the ongoing poker reference, but I still wanted a seat at the table. I could choose to fold. Or to bluff. So, I decided I'd have to work on my poker face.

The only hope and advice from doctors and the internet was to rest. Then rest some more.

Be still.

Be quiet.

And I assure you, I must be desperate to try those two things.

And I am pretty sure God was laughing, because those are things I am even worse at than receiving or playing poker. I have watched more TV in the last three weeks than I have in the last three years.

And slowly the stillness helped.

I do not know if it will last. But I keep praying that it does.

There is a small metal plate that just doesn't feel quite right beneath my skin.

Hair that tickles as it grows back and stitches that will eventually dissolve.

And for those of you that like a happy ending, I can't promise you one. But I do have a much happier now. The swelling has subsided. I do not take any pain medicine stronger than Tylenol and I have gone a little over an entire week without a single shock. That side of my face still feels sore and tingly after I have done more than I should, but that is easy to handle and a gentle reminder to stay in my pajamas. To talk less and listen more. My husband leans in to kiss me and my body still flinches and my head wants to turn. Someone says something funny, and I tell them not to make me laugh. Because those were things that used to hurt. It will take me a while to let that sink in. That I can kiss my husband and that I can laugh without pain. I am more thankful for that than Netflix or pajama pants.

"THE LORD WILL FIGHT for you, you need only to be still,$_{24}$" I am reminded again.

I lie in my bed being still...which is so hard for a girl who loves a good fight.

And I think I have learned.

Stillness.

Desperate.

Overwhelming gratitude.

Stillness. I'm starting to get used to wearing my pjs in public (OK, I did that before).

Desperate because I think that is where you actually start to truly pray and hope — when the options have run out.

Overwhelmed with the kind of thankfulness that only happens when you cannot pay a favor back. At least not any time soon.

I used to make short lists of things I was thankful for every day, and in the last year or so I have forgotten this practice. The other day I figured I should write some thank you cards. For the people who brought me food. Or watched my kids. Or packed and unpacked my house. Sent flowers or fruit. Prayed for me. For cupcakes that literally made me cry. And my list went all the way down the paper and well onto the back. And this overwhelms me in the best way.

My freezer is literally full.

Things are hanging in my closet and on my wall.

My laundry is done.

My dad even had my car detailed because he deemed it unsanitary (he wasn't wrong). My days from the hospital and the week after are blurry, and I can hardly remember most of it, but I do remember lots of people doing what I love best, which is showing up. Over and over, hope knocked on my door, and I couldn't help but let a little in.

AND

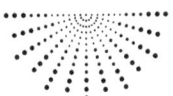

I STARTED WRITING PUBLICLY WHEN MY SON WAS SMALL, back when everyone had a mom blog.

To my surprise people read it, encouraged me, and a few even told me that I should write a book. I inhaled books, loved seeing my words unfold on the page and loved even more the idea that my words could impact someone else. I went to a writing conference and even met with a publisher.

Despite my best efforts back then, I couldn't quite live up to my best supporters' hopes. Then, much as I loved the process, I wasn't sure I knew what my story was yet. I only knew how to pay attention and to ramble, which was close but not quite enough. Even in high school, writing assignments made me uncomfortable. When I wrote I felt naked. As if I only knew how to write the truth, and at that point in my life I wasn't ready for all of the truth.

My story eventually found me, and so did the truth. The first nearly wrecked me, and the other came much later in a quiet office that smelled like essential oils and tea. I'm still learning from it. I was afraid, even in the midst of it, that pain was going to be my story.

Eventually, pain is everyone's story. And frankly not even an interesting one.

Someone who knew me then, complained about her own level of pain, and ended with the caveat that of course it was nothing like mine. Hogwash, pain is pain. It isn't a badge of honor. Only this awful thing that we all share, eventually.

I tried again, a decade later, to write my story. This time around I had a much better idea of who I was and what I had to say. I knew and trusted in my voice, but I still struggled. I found myself just moving words when I had expected them to finally pour out.

I think because I was telling the wrong story. Which makes me ask: if pain isn't the story, then what is? In a kinder moment to myself, I think maybe it is strength. I want to see myself as strong, but I hesitate, some part of me misremembering a Sunday School half-truth. The song we sang over and over as kids, "They are weak, *but He* is strong".

Somehow making weakness seem closer to God. But that wasn't quite the line Paul gave us in 2 Corinthians. "When I am weak, *then I am* strong.[25]" Weakness builds strength, not diminishes it. There is no favor in being weak. Only opportunity. It is where the story starts, but not where it ends.

Even before I had a scar from brain surgery sliding behind my left ear, I had found the idea of *kintsugi* beautiful. Kintsugi is the Japanese art of repairing broken pottery with powdered gold. The cracks become the centerpiece. The few times I've tried to glue something back together, my hope has always been that the glue was clear and seams pressed close enough together that no one would notice.

Kintsugi does the opposite. The repair shimmers on full display, making the piece far more beautiful than it was before. I hide my scars while this form of art gives them the stage. That is about the bravest thing I can imagine.

Most days I do feel strong. I have had to persevere with courage.

I want to see my scars as beautiful rather than sometimes just evidence of being broken.

And that isn't the story either. My husband makes beautiful things with his hands, but I mostly only use words. However, on a whim I ordered a kintsugi kit off of Etsy, thinking I'd make a few Christmas gifts from it. I didn't pay enough attention to realize I was ordering from Europe, and the kit showed up in February instead of December. Just another reminder that gifts, especially in the form of broken things, often take their sweet time.

THE PICTURE online showed a beautiful cup with dramatic gold veins throughout. I thought maybe the kit would come with some pottery pieces for me to restore, and that my finished product would look just like the picture.

Instead, it came with gold powder, a brush, instructions, and some glue. Pottery not included.

I had far too many coffee cups to fit on the shelf, but I still hesitated to try it out.

Because I realized what I'd have to do. Before I could glue something back together with gold, making it stronger and more beautiful, first *it would have to be broken*. My teenagers would have loved the opportunity to take a hammer to some of my favorite mugs, but I was more hesitant. Not that I love my cups that much, but because I understood the symbolism.

I don't want to shatter to restore.

I don't want to be broken to be made beautiful.

I don't want to be made weak to be made strong.

I want to skip that step. I want to skip the pain and the brokenness and the waiting and the being put back together. I only want the beauty and the strength.

But I'm starting to realize that those things come last. Or more likely the middle, because I hope I live a life long enough and full enough to do it all over again.

I put on the gloves and mixed my gold and epoxy. My daughter showed up. I was glad to have company and an extra set of hands, because most repairs, in people and pottery, require help. Our first attempt was a little messy. As I suspected, most attempts at this kind of piecing back together can be. We were both amazed that it worked. At how the shimmery lines stood out on the dark cup. The instructions were very clear that this kit was for decorative purposes only.

I couldn't help it. I filled up my cup with water anyway.

Not to drink, but just to see.

It held, and I suspect I will too.

My small box that traveled across a big ocean contained only epoxy and gold powder.

I took a hammer to a teacup. Separately, they were just powder and glue and broken pieces.

Together they made a beautiful reminder that my scars and broken places tell a story of redemption and hope. My story isn't about pain or strength.

It is about pain AND strength.

It is about brokenness AND beauty.

It is about fear AND hope.

All of it is the story.

Mine and everyone else's.

It has been all along.

The beauty is not in the strength or even the gold.

It is in the cracks AND the restoration.

The cross and AND redemption.

My broken, tired, hard heart AND my tender shimmering one.

GROWTH

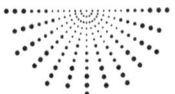

THIS MORNING, AS I WAS LOOKING FOR SOME MEDICAL information, I stumbled across a gallon ziplock bag I'd forgotten about in my bathroom closet. It's marked as a biohazard, and it's full of hair. My hair, shaved from my head. I'm not sure why, but they brought it out to the waiting room during surgery and gave it to my husband. Like a creepy party favor you get for brain surgery. I remembered this bag from the hospital, but I remembered it so much bigger. Back then, in a morphine haze, I saw the bag and reached for the thick section of hair they'd shaved just above my ear down to the base of my neck. Thankfully, they'd left some on top so I could hide it easily. My hair has grown in, but I am still hiding it.

Hair grows slow. Half an inch a month. My son was born with a thick head of black hair that eventually grew in blond and constantly needs to be cut. I expected the same when my daughter was born, but she came out screaming, bald and so pale you could almost see through her. And she stayed that way. On her first birthday, people told me to be patient, that her hair would grow. On her second birthday, they told me to be patient, that her hair would grow. On her third birthday, I could almost pull a few hairs into a tiny ponytail.

When she was four, she started asking me to braid it like the girls in her class, but that was impossible. For dance recitals I had to get creative to pull those fine wisps into a bun. The struggle was real. Her hair is still thin but wild, still not growing at the usually slow rate. She took about seven years to grow a respectable ponytail. It took a while, but eventually it grew in.

My son is the tiniest. Really. The smallest kid in his entire school. His friends tower over him. I worry he will get picked on or shoved into lockers, but he seems to hold his own. He is in the second percentile on the growth charts. He was so sick as a toddler that I worry his growth is permanently stunted. I keep waiting for his pediatrician to bring up growth hormones or refer us to an endocrinologist. She never does. She says she makes referrals only when growth stalls, but my son's slowly and steadily creeps up on the graph. He is growing, just not at the same rate as everyone else.

Growth has its own timetable.

I should throw this bag of hair away. It is weird and gross, but I just can't. It is this tangible reminder of things I have lost. Things I hope one day will be returned to me. I think of pulling out another ziplock back and filling it with a list of all the things lost. I imagine the bag overflowing. I have lost: hair, thousands and thousands of dollars I don't want to add up, the ability to talk or smile or eat and laugh some days without excruciating pain, being unafraid, running, playing sports, not taking a ridiculous amount of pills, all kinds of hours in bedrest and exhausted coffee/alcohol trips, 15-20 pounds I keep losing and gaining right back when I feel OK again, chewing gum, the ability to sing at church and pray without a fight, a few friends I really don't miss anyway, professional confidence and opportunities, dozens of parties, dinners and happy hours I just didn't feel up to, hours and hours to sitting in waiting rooms, concerts, late bedtimes, never asking for help and all the layers of my heart I haven't seen in so long that I barely recognize them now.

Then I start another list. It is much shorter, but I think more important: faith, resilience, my favorite people, words, humor, hot tea, all kinds of things on the first list I am afraid will hurt but I sometimes do anyway. I could probably add more to both lists.

This morning the bag looked smaller and flatter than I remembered it from July. Just like I remember how much I have lost as bigger than it really is. My hair has grown back thick and full. What was lost in that department has been fully renewed. I've read somewhere that sometimes when people lose all their hair to chemo or other things, it grows back differently. A slightly different color or different thickness. Not always but sometimes.

My hair has grown back, but so many other things that were lost have yet to be returned to me.

I start to think that maybe they are just different.

So different I don't even recognize them.

Maybe they aren't here yet.

Maybe they are just on their own timetable.

TAKE COURAGE

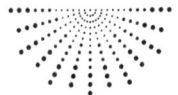

My sophomore English teacher kicked off the school year by reading Anne Sexton on the first day of school, a poem called "Courage,[26]" Fifteen-year-old me did not care much for poetry or even English class. Poetry has grown on me over the years, but I don't miss memorizing Shakespeare or taking standardized tests or the huge literature book that took up most of the real estate in my maroon JanSport backpack.

I wrapped my book carefully with a brown grocery sack that by the end of the year was covered in markers, drawings, and scratch-outs of boys' names. Before I turned my book in at the end of the year, I took a box cutter and carefully cut out one page. I carved out the page with the poem we had read on the first day. I'd never intentionally defaced a textbook before. I always tried to erase my stray marks, and I never dog-eared the pages. I'm not sure what exactly motivated me to carefully cut out an entire page. I liked the photograph, the close-up of a girl full of freckles. She did not look that different from me, but likely it was the way the poem felt in my mouth when I read it.

"Your courage was a small coal you kept swallowing..."

Looking back, I think I wanted to take that courage with me.

I wanted to fold it up and put it in my back pocket.

I wish finding courage was as easy as landing on the right page in my literature book. I wish that it could be stolen or tucked away. I lost that torn page somewhere between 1993 and today. I've lost courage over and over again, but I've also found it. Often like that day, in someone else's words.

When my own children went to school, I'd often repeat the same thing when I dropped them off each morning. I'd remind them to be brave and kind and do more than the minimum. Now they just roll their eyes, so I don't say it as often. I always listed brave first, but I had it wrong. I figured bravery and courage were one and the same. However, they are not interchangeable. Bravery is often associated with instinct or a lack of fear, doing a hard thing without thinking or being afraid. Courage is being afraid and doing the hard thing anyway.

I'll take courage over bravery any day.

If you try to find verses on bravery in the Bible, you will find that verse after verse tells us "to be of good courage.[27]" When his followers see Jesus walking on water, he responds by telling them in Matthew 14, "Take courage! It is I.[28]" I'm not exactly sure that ripping words out of textbooks is exactly what Jesus had in mind, but I love that the verse says to "take" courage. Courage is not always something we have innately inside us but a fuel we can find, borrow, and keep. Sexton's poem tells us that courage is love and comfort and shown in little ways, and these are the things I now tuck away.

I've faced some difficult seasons that the fifteen-year-old me never would have imagined: chronic illness, loss, and uncertainty. Most often I did so with someone else's figurative courage in my pocket. Their prayers. Their belief in me. Their encouragement and comfort.

Recently I had to have a few hard conversations in an area of my life where I do not feel brave. I worried about this conversation for days, trying to strategize my best approach.

My pockets were empty.

I felt like that high school freckled girl again in literature class, stealing words because I did not know how to find my own. I printed out a poem and I put it in my pocket, but I didn't stop there. I wrote down a verse reminding me to take courage. I printed a kind email from a friend. I felt their edges as I asked the difficult questions. These words were not magic. They did not get me the answers I was hoping for, but I realized that if I can take courage, then maybe I can also give it. Give love and comfort and kind words.

Give courage and take it. Steal it if you have to.

THE MIDDLE

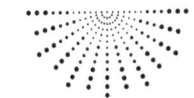

Lately, I've been doing something unusual: staying up and watching baseball. Sure, I love going to baseball games (mostly because I love nachos), but I rarely watch them on TV. My hometown team in the World Series will change my Netflix queue.

A few nights ago, on Game two of the World Series, I went to bed when it didn't look good for my home team. Call me a two-percenter all you want, but my days start early. The next morning while getting coffee, I was shocked to see a Rangers win taking up a full page spread on a newspaper another customer had left discarded on the table. I fell asleep and missed the comeback.

Even more recently, my average college team took down the #3 team in the nation, but I had gone to bed at half time. Again, I was worn out and exhausted. I love to root for my alma mater, but a rain delay and two trunk or treats with a Jawa and Rainbow Brite on too much candy had done me in. When my husband came to bed, well after midnight, he informed me that they'd held the lead for one of the biggest upsets in school history. I had slept through it, again.

Sure, I can watch the highlights or read about it in the paper, but that isn't quite the same thing. Reading about it after the fact doesn't make your heart pound, and you certainly don't jump off the couch cheering. Knowing how it ends somehow takes away part of the excitement.

I read somewhere that the plot of most traditional musicals is simple: Boy meets girl. Boy gets girl. Boy loses girl. Boy gets girl back. How lame would the story be if we ended it after the first act? Or we left after the breakup scene? How different would most books or movies be if we stopped in the middle? Or, like me, went to sleep before it was over?

I've read and listened to enough talks about writing to learn that a critical element to any story is conflict. In other words: the middle. I hate that. I want to start at the beginning and skip to the end and avoid the messy, long, hard middle. The part where we have to go to the store. Or the kids are sick. Or the tire is flat. Or I watch the same episode of *Gilmore Girls* for the tenth time. Or we get on each other's nerves. I'm even going to go out on a limb and say that conflict is critical not just to a story, but also to a relationship. Show me a married couple who never fights, and I'm willing to bet they never speak.

The middle is never the most intriguing part of the story.

The beginning tries to hook you, and the ending tries to make you cry with either joy or sadness and resolve everything. Those two chapters get all the big scenes and moments and the fanciest words. But the middle is really where the story is.

Most of the time we are living in the middle. In the conflict. Or the boring stretch. Or where a character (the one in the story or even just our own) is being developed. The middle requires patience and hope. The middle is where we grow, even when it is painful.

We long for beginnings and ends. But we can't have a story without the middle.

And I am not naïve enough to think that they all have happy endings.

Some of those subplots are still going to be tragedies.

The boy might not get the girl back.

Games are lost.

Healing doesn't always happen.

Some middles are really ends that lead to even better beginnings.

I'm learning to appreciate the middle. I'm realizing that it is an important part of the story. Even if it isn't the one I'm trying to tell. And that if the middle is hard, I just need to hold on to enough hope to make it until the next act. Or at least stay awake long enough to see the end of the game.

BEFORES AND AFTERS

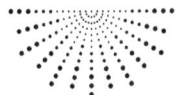

SPRING OF 2022.

I've seen a lot of people posting pictures from this time two years ago. There are posts asking people to share the last pre-pandemic photo on their camera roll of when things were "normal."

My picture for today exactly two years ago was my "new office" (my couch), my kids fighting, and my grocery-store run when I couldn't find any meat or toilet paper but bought wine and Oreos.

Some things have drastically changed in those two years, and some are exactly the same. A few days before, we had been skiing in Taos. There were whispers of a virus, and a few borders were shutting down, but we had no idea what was coming. Most of us have these before and after pictures on our phone of pre-and post-Covid worlds. It is a before and after that the entire world shares, though we have all had varying experiences.

But it is also a good reminder that everyone has their own befores and afters. Ones that are not shared with the planet and rarely posted on social media. They have before the diagnosis, before the phone call, before the loss.

I had my own version of that play out this week. I accidentally stumbled on my last "normal" photo. I was looking for an old Halloween picture on my phone. I scrolled through Instagram to find it, going back several years, and landed on one of me in a dental chair. I froze. It was dated November 8, 2013. The caption under it was aiming for a laugh. Except that now I wasn't laughing. This was a very out of character post for me (because usually I only post pictures of my kids, dog, books or trips), but for some reason I felt the need to document it. A student handed me a blow pop on our way out of the building for a first period fire drill. I bit into my sucker and my molar split in two, and I carried half of it in my pocket back into the building. It didn't hurt, but I was concerned about how much it would hurt my wallet. My dentist got me in that afternoon and told me that I was lucky, that he thought he could save me from a root canal. He took a long time repairing the damage and fitting me for a crown. I spent almost two hours with my jaw craned open and the drill vibrating.

Something in me shifted that day; it would just take me a while to realize it. I wrote some snarky comment under the Instagram post about how expensive that blow pop ended up being. A few days later, I got my first tiny shock. It happened each morning for weeks as I put on my makeup. They were so slight that at first that I thought maybe I had imagined them, until the next day when it would happen all over again. Each time I thought, "I should ask a doctor about this," but then I would forget again. The shocks were on the opposite side of my face from my new crown, so I didn't connect the two for years. That is the last post of when things were "normal" for me.

Several pictures after that image came a photo of me with my closest friends celebrating a birthday one month later. Earlier that night we had tubed down the indoor ice exhibits, ordered good food and wine and laughed until my face literally hurt. However, what I most remember about that night was that I almost spilled my wine glass on our waitress as the electrical shocks got stronger. My once-a-morning zap suddenly happened at dinner. Over and over and over again, at a pain level that could no longer be ignored.

There are sixteen pictures on my phone between the dentist's office and that dinner. Sixteen images between being broken and realizing it. They are of my kids' soccer games, playing in the fountain, books, post-race celebrations, friends, my crazy kids, great meals, and adventures.

I finally made that doctor's appointment. I was misdiagnosed more than once. Given all kinds of pills that didn't help. One doctor suggested a psychologist before another finally recognized my classic symptoms and sent me straight to a well-known neurologist. He gave me pills that immediately worked. They made me sleepy, run slower, gain a few pounds and sometimes forgetful. But I only took a few, and some days I'd skip them all together.

The photos continue. And they are so fun to look through. My kids are joyful. We go on amazing trips. I run a half marathon. I do crazy things at school. I spend time with my favorite people.

Then years later there is a third picture that gives me pause. This one is dated July 2015. It is of my mismatched socks sticking out from a hospital bed before they wheeled me off for surgery. My caption this time was only one word: "Ready." But I had no idea what I thought I was ready for, because I can assure you, I was not. Between the dinner where I realized something was wrong and the hospital, there are literally hundreds of photos. This stage where I went from managed to desperate is full of races, vacations, birthdays, soccer games, dress-up days, girls' nights and cute kids.

Even during pain that led me to cut a hole in my head, I literally couldn't pick a hundred favorite images. And then I look at images after surgery. It took me years to find any kind of real relief. However, from most of these pictures you cannot tell. There are no more defining images. I can remember enough to know that there was hesitation behind some of these pictures.

Mountains I was afraid to climb in case of an attack. Trips that I was uncertain of but took anyway. Concerts that maybe I didn't make it all the way through. But I can't find an image and say that is the last one where I was really hurting. Or that is the last picture of when I was afraid all the time. Or the last picture of when I took fistfuls of pills. It is too hard to tell or remember.

The healing was so slow and gradual that I almost missed the miracle.

Even my after images are still in a state of in-between. And I certainly can't find an image in there and say, this one, this is the one where I started living again — because I had never stopped. I remember those years as a painful blur, but frankly my images tell a different story. There are still hundreds of pictures of races, trips, dinners, adventures, birthdays, graduations, weddings, my kids doing their favorite things while I am there to witness it. They are smiling their faces off. More hikes than my kids have ever wanted to go on. Oceans and lakes. Mountains (and volcanoes) climbed. Literally and figuratively.

I know that life on social media isn't real. It is curated and edited. But these reminders are very much real. The joy is there, even if there was a layer of pain or medication underneath them. At their worst they are incomplete. But so is looking at only the three images: the dentist, the dinner and the hospital. There are hundreds and hundreds of others in-between and after.

I've also learned that life is a series of before and afters. None of us are lucky enough to only have one. It isn't the before pictures that matter nearly as much as the ones that follow.

I challenge anyone to go back and find a before picture from COVID. To think about how hard it was, how much we lost and whom we lost. Grieve and remember.

But keep scrolling. I found pictures of Zoom meetings with friends I had not seen in years. Sidewalk chalk. Hundreds of meals outside. Hikes. Birthday parades. Weird first days of school. Vaccines. Vacations. Masks and plenty of memories I want to keep. Having a before we can all share is also a good place to be aware of the befores and afters people carry and keep to themselves. It is an opportunity to be a little gentler with other peoples' stories. It is an opportunity to be a little gentler with your own. It is an opportunity to acknowledge not only the pain of before but the unexpected joy that you can still find after.

AND SO SHE DID

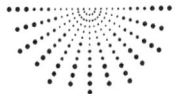

This morning a friend came by to give me a thoughtful gift. She's been in the middle of a particularly hard loss, and I've had the blessing to try and be a good friend through it.

She gave me a bracelet that had the phrase "She believed she could, so she did" engraved in the middle. She bought this particular bracelet with this particular phrase because she felt like it encapsulated me.

I was touched, but I'm not so sure about the phrase. Maybe on the outside that looks true. I have tackled some hard things across the last decade of our friendship. It looks like I've set my mind to achieve some difficult tasks and have accomplished them.

I believed I could run a half marathon, so I did.

Except I trained for a year and wanted to quit on almost every single run.

I believed I could get another degree, so I applied to school and I did.

Except the reality involved buckets of tears, missed social events and loads of help. It took years or hard work and dozens of pep talks to overcome my doubt.

I believed I could heal, so I had brain surgery and now my pain is much more manageable.

Except this type of healing took years, my entire savings and pain that occasionally still lands me in bed for the day.

In January I decided to really commit and work on my hopes to write a book.

I've invested my time, money and energy into this work. I made a website, committed to a semi-regular newsletter, read books and took online workshops. Even before I could say I had a book to offer the world, I had articles published both online and in print. I've even gotten paid for it. I've had more than my share of rejection emails, but I've also hit many of the milestones I was hoping for.

It looks like I believed I could write, so I did.

But here is the honest truth: I'm not sure I ever believed I could.

I only believed it was worth a try. I believed I was worth investing in.

I believed I should go out swinging rather than simply hoping.

I didn't know if I could run the distance until I crossed the finish line. I didn't know if I'd ever get through my dissertation until my committee chair called me doctor.

Despite having had a short season of progress and small wins, I'm still not sure I can be a writer. I am hitting goals, and each time there is a small celebration, a validation, and then another slew of questions and doubts. I wonder what milestone I will need to hit to believe that I can. What will I need to accomplish to really own the phrasing on my bracelet?

A book in my hands or on shelves? A large enough payout to sustain my writing? Thousands of followers on social media or on my mailing list? Somehow, I doubt it. I keep moving the finish line. Some days we all think we are imposters.

Maybe the bracelet should have said, "She was full of doubt and uncertainty but showed up and did the work anyway because she had just enough hope and encouragement to keep trying." I'm not sure that one would fit around my wrist, but it is certainly closer to the truth.

I believe **after** I hit submit, send or post rather than before.

I didn't believe I could, so I did.

I did so that I could believe.

Sometimes I wonder if my faith is the same. If it is a muscle or a habit that takes practice. Not a certainty we innately hold, but a belief we carry that is more of a small hope and continual showing up. Today I look down at my wrist and choose to believe that I'm not an imposter. I believe that I am a writer, not because of any goals I have met but simply because I am spending my Sunday morning typing away. I believe, because I'm doing the work. I'm getting better. I'm putting myself out there. Tomorrow I'm likely to question and forget again.

Either way I hope to show up, regardless of what I believe.

THE UNDERSTORY

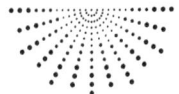

OVER SPRING BREAK I VISITED SAN FRANCISCO WITH MY family. We watched the sea lions on the pier, heard the parrots on Telegraph Hill, felt the Golden Gate Bridge sway in the wind, had our trolley get stuck going up a hill, dipped our toes in the freezing bay, hiked up thousands of stairs, took a night tour of Alcatraz, wound our way both up and down Lombard Street. We ate all the things and easily walked over ten miles each day (more than once in the wind and rain).

I've visited the Bay area several times, but until this trip I've never made it out to Muir woods. The redwoods had all the magic and then some. Muir smells like Christmas, looks like Endor and makes you feel small in the best possible, holiest of ways. When we visit a park or museum, each member of my family responds differently. My husband reads every informational sign or marker. My daughter plows ahead leading the group (her middle name is Harper and we thought we'd call her Scout; the name never quite stuck, but the action did), and my son lags way behind taking a hundred nature photos. I rarely read the information placards and prefer my photos with people (or dogs) in them. One sign, however, caught my eye as I was leaving the park:

"Protect the Understory"

I knew the term overstory — the huge canopies — thanks to the novel by Richard Powers[29], but had never heard of the understory, and the phrasing stuck with me. "Redwoods are the tallest trees on Earth but have surprisingly shallow roots."

Actually, the sign was being modest; redwoods are not just the tallest tree but the tallest living thing on Earth. I read this and assumed the signage was asking us to protect the shallow roots. Like the placard suggested, I had thought that these massive trees that go so far up would also anchor themselves with an impressive depth. According to the U.S. National Park Service[30], the tallest tree in the Muir woods is 258 feet tall. These trees can weigh over 6,000 tons, but only grow six to twelve vertical feet of roots to hold them in place.

Our trip to the coast did not line up with Mother Nature's finest. Most days were cold, rainy, and windy. My umbrella did not survive my walk to lunch at the farmer's market, and tree branches littered the San Francisco sidewalk. Cleaning crews worked to clean up the windy wreckage as the sun finally came out for a long stretch on our drive to the airport. I wondered how the redwoods fared. Turns out they can handle much more wind than me or my umbrella, not because of deep roots but because of a wide support network. Redwoods grow up, but the roots grow out and intertwine with neighboring trees. They grow huge horizontal root nets up to a hundred feet out. Alone, this wouldn't be enough to anchor it in a storm, but redwoods don't grow in isolation. They thrive in groves where their shallow roots intertwine and even fuse together with their neighbors. They literally hold each other up with enough strength to stay put through most of what nature throws at it for hundreds and possibly thousands of years.

The sign wasn't asking us to protect the shallow roots, but rather all the networks and connections to the other trees. In other words, it was protecting relationships. I might be pulling too hard on this metaphor, but it made me wonder what relationships hold me up, and what am I doing to protect them? If it is enough to keep a 258-foot-tall, majestic tree standing, I suppose the same will do for my 67 inches.

That is lesson enough, but I did more research. The understory is not the roots but all the smaller growth at the base of these giants. A forest is made up of three layers: the overstory (or canopy), the understory and the forest floor. The understory is the underlying layer between the tallest trees and the forest floor. It is made up of specialty shade-tolerant shrubs and trees (such as dogwood) and young canopy trees. Some of these younger canopy trees can persist in the understory for decades until an opening allows room for them to grow. Hope is in the understory and in the trees there just waiting for enough light to become the overstory.

Sometimes I feel like I'm not moving fast enough, that I'm behind. That I should be further along in my career or in my writing or in my own healing. I mean, who doesn't relate to the line in the song "Wait for It" from Hamilton:

"I'm not falling behind or running late. I'm not standing still: I am lying in wait.[31]*"*

Much of the understory is lying in wait. Waiting for the space and sun and the right conditions to grow and thrive. This is how the redwoods reach such great heights. They have been protecting their understory. They have been growing roots, not down but out. And so instead of feeling behind or pushing through when I'm not quite ready, maybe it would be better to make like a tree. Focus on the relationships that hold me up, wait for the right conditions to flourish and protect my understory.

MORE THAN I CAN HANDLE

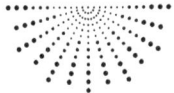

I WENT TO CHURCH TODAY FOR THE FIRST TIME IN OVER A year. I don't remember the last time I attended. The specifics didn't feel important in the moment. I have long forgotten the songs we sang. The sermon. What I wore or whom we ate with afterward. Maybe if I'd known church would take years to look like church again, I would have paid more attention.

I never quite embraced the online version of church. It is hard to build community apart. Despite my best intentions, I fell out of habit. Sure, I attended an Easter service in the giant auditorium.

I occasionally streamed services into my living room.

I worshiped outside. I joined an online Bible study. I sat week after week in the sanctuary for Confirmation, but I longed for a "normal Sunday." I have missed the hard pews. The familiar faces. The quiet. The loudness. The emptiness. The uncertainty. The longing. The made right. The not yet. The with-you-ness.

When I finally return, it feels anything but normal. I wait for someone to hand me a bulletin as I walk in. This used to be my job. I was an usher, greeter and I served communion.

There are no more bulletins, only a QR code taped to the pew in front of me. Someone hands me a ziplock bag with a Hawaiian roll and a pre-sealed thimble of grape juice inside. The holy elements bagged up like a school snack.

In our absence, the crowd has changed. I only see a few familiar faces, some still covered in masks. I slipped a piece of paper and a pen in my purse before I left the house to take notes on, but the Bibles and hymnals are gone and there is nothing to press down against. The rest of me feels the same, unsure what is solid anymore. The songs don't move me, the message doesn't land. It feels like what I longed for is missing. I wanted it to be what it was, but so much of the world has shifted, of course my heart has too. The first twenty minutes I only feel disappointment and loss.

Then the pastor wraps up early. He says, close your Bibles, the teaching is over.

And then he has a seat. Still on stage. But a seat. This is as unusual as the QR codes and ziplock communion. Now we are just going to talk, he says.

"What do you do when everyone is in need? What do you do when you look around and everyone is hurting, and few of us have anything left to give?"

I no longer notice all the people I don't know, and I pull to the edge of my seat.

This is why I am here.

"Hurt people hurt people," he reminds us.

I often say that stressed people respond in stress (usually to myself as I respond to angry emails). And I have been so damn stressed, I am likely the giver and the receiver of this right now. I've hesitated to reach out to my community because they are in so much need themselves. I've been busy trying to be community, when I desperately need it. Community isn't something you are, it is something that you are a part of.

My closest coworker just buried her mother.

Another spent the week at MD Anderson with her sister until they sent her home without treatment. One of my closest friend's husbands is moving out on Monday, and another currently quarantined. Another's spouse is not responding to his second stem cell treatment.

And that is just this week. I want so badly to show up for them, but I don't know how to show up for myself. I have multiple teachers in the hospital. There is not enough staff, even in health.

My own office is spread thin. I can't get in the bathroom because a newly volun-told virtual teacher is teleconferencing with a parent. I can't get my drink out of the fridge because another virtual teacher is recording a video in the kitchen and someone else is crying in the stairwell.

We are all carrying a lot. It is too much for anyone to bear.

My lot isn't special. It isn't particularly big or heavy. But I still haven't quite figured out how to manage it, much less try to carry anyone else's. It hasn't stopped me from trying, but it has stopped me from sleeping.

The pastor says that at this level of need and stress and grief, we are all basically walking around as the worst versions of ourselves. It is easy to notice the worst in others, but harder to own mine. On the screen is no longer a Bible verse, but instead a suicide hotline and then the emergency pastor number. He tells us all to get out our phones and save those numbers in our contacts.

We are all empty. We are all struggling.

Then he tells us to do something that I've heard three times now in the last few days.

The repetition is not lost on me. "Pray for the people you don't want to pray for."

Followed up with, and I'm paraphrasing, "Meet needs, your neighbors' and your own, as best you can, but recognize how little many of us have to give right now. Offer grace if it is all you have to give, and that is enough." He offers more hope, of course, and has some suggestions on how to fill some of the emptiness.

But this honesty and struggle is what actually draws me in. We can't feel hopeful if we don't start with the truth: that it is OK to be in need right now, whether big or small; that it is OK not to know how to meet the needs of others.

It is OK to be empty. It is OK to call your therapist. Or your pastor. That community matters even in that. Even when we are all tired or cranky or numb or afraid.

Even when we are the worst versions of ourselves.

When we are hurt or afraid or anxious, self-protection or withdrawal is sometimes what we move into. Or at least I do, but to resist. I'm reminded of a Brene Brown podcast early in the pandemic[32]. "Love is the last thing we need to ration right now." It does not run out, even when we do.

He then stands and offers us communion. There is no chalice or loaf of bread at the front for his Thanksgiving liturgy. Instead, he breaks a small roll in half. The same kind I have in a baggie next to me. Christ's body broken for broken me in a room full of broken people.

And for this short moment, *I am full*.

Years have passed and much of what I'd considered to be normal church has returned.

There are bulletins and bread pressed into my open hands. Yet many of us started asking new questions about purpose. Those of us that fell out of habit wondered if it was worth picking up again. Every once in a while, it still feels again like everything is hitting all at once, and I hear the often-misquoted adage about "God never giving you more than you can handle" play in my head. Which is of course not at all what Paul said[33].

Pandemic or no pandemic, I've been stressed and overwhelmed and felt every bit more than I can handle. Each time I've been required to let something go. To ask for help. To toss out my calendar. To rely on others. Hope is not a one-man job. Hope is not confined to a church building, but it helps every time I find myself broken in a room full of broken people. When we have been given too much to handle, we are instead held.

IN A NAME

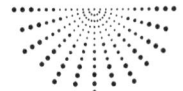

"In English my name means hope. In Spanish it means too many letters. It means sadness, it means waiting. It is like the number nine. A muddy color. It is the Mexican records my father plays on Sunday mornings when he is shaving, songs like sobbing."

-Sandra Cisneros, *The House on Mango Street* 34

For a writing workshop, an author read an excerpt from *House on Mango Street*. I have not read this book since early high school. I liked it then, but I suspect much was lost to my youth. Lost on the fifteen-year-old worried more about her bangs and the boy sitting next to her than the narrator's voice. So when I hear this passage now, it hits differently. It settles into me like a smooth stone in my pocket. A comfort and a heaviness.

She asks us to write our own versions. Start with, *my name means*...and simply write for a few minutes. Michelle is a plain enough name. No one mispronounces it, and only occasionally does someone misspell it. Sometimes it shows up on the keychains or nameplates they sell in gas stations. There were rarely other Michelles in my class, so I never had to use an initial. The Beatles even sang a song with the same refrain.

My name has never quite felt like it fit, but I've worn it anyway, like pants that are a little too tight and I'm happy to peel off the second I get home. I know where my name comes from, and like for the narrator, it is a connection to a grandmother. Her maiden name was Schell, and I suppose my name is a nod to that. Unlike Cisneros, I don't have stories about her being a horse of a woman. I barely know my family history. Although I know where the name comes from, I do not know what it actually means.

A QUICK GOOGLE search remedies that. The name Michelle has French (like the Beatles song) and Hebrew roots that mean, "**One who resembles God.**" And I'm not quite sure what to do with that; my name feels like it fits even less now. Because I do not feel much like I resemble God. Unless God spills her coffee. Or loses her car keys. Or her patience. Unless God swears and laughs just a little too loudly and has questionable tastes in music. Unless God hits snooze and can never remember to move the clothes from the washer to the dryer before they grow a mildewy smell.

I pause in my humanity and shortcomings for a minute and think, what if it is true?

Despite my tendencies, I am forced to call up my best qualities rather than my questionable ones. I struggle to receive compliments and even more so to give them to myself.

One who resembles God begs the question: what parts of me resemble a creator?

The me who stitches words together and scratches them out.

The me who lays parts of her heart out there that still feel a little tender.

The me who writes with hopes that a reader will see me but also themselves.

I'm no longer in school. I do not have to write out my name at the top of worksheets or headings on blue and white notebook paper. Even my email signature is automatic. But still, I give my name to the barista for my coffee. I sign it on the bottom of sympathy cards. I scribble an unreadable signature next to my name for attendance at a meeting that will likely be longer than I want. I use my finger to spell it out on screens with every purchase I make. I type it next to titles of essays.

And now it will be hard to unsee the meaning.

One who resembles God.

It is more of a hope and a reminder for me than a promise on my end.

Regardless of what our name means, we are all image-bearers.

We are all creators hoping to reflect parts of ourselves and parts of our Father.

The one who named you and the one who stitched you together.

And for the first time, my name feels like it fits.

NEW SHOES

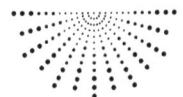

Recently I went to the local running store and let them charge a ridiculous amount for a new pair of running shoes. I used to run, just like I used to do lots of things, but lately I have been slow to get off the couch. Let's be honest: this season has been a long one, and I've been slow to do a lot of things that are good for me. My old shoes are wearing thin, and nothing motivates like a new pair of kicks.

I quickly found my brand and style of choice and asked the worker to bring them in my size. The owner spoke up from the back, "So you are picking your shoes out based on how they look?" I pulled my own foot into her view. I showed her a similar pair in teal, well worn, with the big toe scuffed all the way through. The model was a few years old, and I needed a fresh start.

"Nope. These are my brand, but I'm open to your suggestions."

Runners are very particular about their shoes.

I tell her I need something to absorb a lot of the impact.

I tell her that I overpronate just a little.

I tell her that my knees suck, but I never mention the hole in my head.

I tell her I'm a distance runner, not a speed runner.

Even though the farthest I've run in a year is two miles. Currently, I can't even do one.

They fit. Of course they do. I've bought this same brand, same size, at least a half dozen times. The price tag should make me hesitate, but I give her all my money without flinching.

Buying these shoes feels a little ridiculous. They are a luxury I can't really afford. I barely run; I probably don't need these fancy shoes. I'm too slow for the shoes of a serious runner. I could go to Academy and buy two or three pairs of shoes for this price. But these shoes, or at least similar ones, have carried me hundreds of miles. Across finish lines.

My heels have bled. More than one toenail fell off. I've pushed myself when I wanted to quit.

I've done hard things in shoes like these.

These are the shoes of a runner. Albeit a slow one.

And I am hopeful still.

Maybe I can't run far, but I am still in the damn race.

They are beautiful shoes.

I wore them yesterday to the grocery store and got two compliments.

But even better, I laced them up, grabbed my headphones and hit an actual trail.

I can't tell you how many times I've restarted the Couch to 10K app.

In the last year alone, four times. The farthest I've made it is week 6. I have not quit for lack of motivation or discipline.

Some might say that is four times I have not met my goal.

Some might say it is four times that I have given up.

I say it is four times I've been hopeful.

It is four times that I've listened to my body even when I didn't want to.

And four times I've started over again.

It is four times I've slowed down. Four times I've rested.

It is four times I've done what I loved, despite all the reasons to stay on the couch.

I'm not so sure finishing is even the goal anymore.

In a bottom drawer, I have medals and a few trophies from races I used to run.

I was never fast, but I always finished, and I occasionally even won.

Then, several years ago, I had brain surgery and a chronic pain condition that made even walking painful.

I put the medals out of sight. I recycled all the race shirts.

They were just a sad reminder.

But I never stopped buying running shoes.

I never stopped hoping.

Today I am slow.

But I still run.

And then I walk.

And then I run again.

My head starts to tingle. Not the best sign, but it could be worse.

I slow down. Heck, I can barely breathe anyway.

And I do it again the next day.

These shoes are worth every overpriced penny that I paid.

Because they remind me what I can do.

Because they remind me that it doesn't matter if I run or walk as long as I keep going.

Because they remind me that I can always begin again.

BLOODWORK

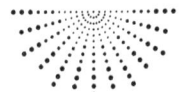

THE NURSE CALLED WITH MY BLOODWORK SEVERAL WEEKS ago. My numbers have been high since my twenties, even when I was running twenty miles a week. Genetics are not in my favor, neither are the extra pounds, stress eating and canceling my gym membership. My cholesterol is high. My triglycerides are through the roof. My blood sugar is always on the edge. This time, I fell over the edge. The nurse told me to call my primary. That my numbers have hit the "time to make some major life changes" range.

    I wasn't surprised, but I was not ready. My initial urge was to try and fix things before seeing a doctor. Which is kind of the opposite of a doctor's job, but on brand for me. I made the appointment. I started taking my statins again. I examined what I was eating and reduced some of the bad ideas (sayonara, cupcakes). The biggest change I made: I started running again.

    I am a runner. I have a box of medals, race shirts and a few trophies to prove it. However, in the last decade I've been hit or miss. Mostly miss. Getting back into it has been hard for a handful of reasons. The running is difficult, but harder is the fact that I've lost the muscles for it. This thing that used to be easy is now a strain on every part of my body. My endurance is shot. One mile now feels like twelve. Except, no one is handing me a medal when I finish.

Each day I've been lacing up my sneakers and hitting the trail anyway. It is a lesson in humility but has also been a lesson in hope.

Most people would prefer to compare hope to something happy instead of laborious, but I know better. My hope has not come cheap. Sometimes it is as much a choice as exercise.

I have lived through seasons where hope was all I had, but also seasons where hope felt dangerous. When nothing seemed to be working, when I had tried all the next steps. When the miracle didn't seem to be coming. How do you hold on to hope in those moments when you can't face another disappointment? I read a lot about hope because I was desperate for it, and this verse hit me:

"Not only so, but we also glory in our sufferings, because we know that suffering produces perseverance; perseverance, character; and character, hope.[35]*"*

Hope was last. Not first.

Suffering offers perseverance.

Perseverance builds character.

Eventually, character produces hope.

Hope isn't always what you hold on to during hard things, it is literally the product of the hard thing.

Last Advent season, the pastor started a sermon with a verse about waiting. He asked us to turn our Bibles to Isaiah 40. I can barely get to church with matching shoes on, so I didn't exactly remember a Bible. Instead, I grabbed my phone and typed in the verse.

He started reading.

*"But they that **wait** upon the Lord shall renew their strength; they shall mount up with wings as eagles; they shall run, and not be weary; and they shall walk, and not faint.*[36]*"*

He paused on the word *wait*. And read it again to emphasize the point he was going to make. My phone, however, said something different for the exact same verse: *"but those who **hope** in the Lord will renew their strength... ₃₇"*

A subtle difference in a slightly more modern translation. I flipped between interpretations on my phone and found the words hope and wait used in various versions of the same passage. The pastor kept going, but I was hung up on the idea of hope and waiting being related. The hope was in the waiting, not the renewal. I always thought that hope was something you had or found, not something you grew.

I've been running every day for a few weeks now. I've made it through week 4 on my Couch to 10K app. This app has you walk, then jog, then walk again. Each week the minutes of jogging get longer and longer and the walking shorter and less frequent. The first few weeks you never have to run more than a few minutes before it dings for a reprieve. Those two minutes felt much harder than they should have, but I pushed through until it dinged so I could breathe easy again. Those two minutes grew into twelve and now twenty. I can go farther than I could four weeks ago. I'm slowly building back some endurance. I persevere even when I want to quit. I know that a break is coming. I run and hope for the ding telling me to walk. I am learning when to keep going and when to rest.

Whoever says that hope is easy misleads others. Anyone who offers hopes and prayers flippantly doesn't know what they are promising. Enduring hope is hard earned. Hope is in the waiting. Hope is in the suffering. Hope keeps going. One mile or twenty. It perseveres.

Hope comes from suffering.

Hope comes from waiting.

Hope comes from trying again.

Hope comes from failure not success.

Hope is in the rest that I trust is coming, even when the road still feels long.

Hope doesn't come from answered prayers; instead, I'm starting to think it comes from honest desperate prayers that maybe you aren't even sure anyone is listening to.

For the last month, I wake up each morning and everything aches, because perseverance (and hope) doesn't come without a cost. I will check back in with my doctor soon.

I could have simply "hoped and prayed" that my blood work would improve, but I don't think that is the kind of hope that Paul teaches. Instead, I chose to build endurance. I struggle and sweat and persevere. I'm building hope. One mile and minute at a time.

CHRISTMAS LIGHTS

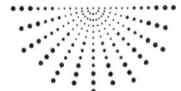

IN MAY, A FRIEND TEXTED ME LATE AT NIGHT, WORRIED about her father's health. She said when it was time that she wanted me to help her write words to honor him and told me precisely what she wanted to convey. It would have been easy for her to get caught up in some of the harder parts of her family's story, but she was crystal clear: she only wanted to talk about grace and redemption.

I never got the chance to help her write it; instead, not many months later, I stood at the front of a church, behind the flowers and her photos, and spoke words that I thought would be for a very different time. Like she had asked, I wrote about grace and redemption, but my hands shook and I spoke with an unsteady voice. These words were now to honor her, and it was a good thing she'd forced me to look for grace and redemption because I struggled to find them on my own. When the service ended, I couldn't face all the lines and the people, and I quickly made my escape from the sanctuary.

Shortly after, my kitchen table filled with friends who had surrounded me in those hard wooden pews. We ate and remembered and caught up and occasionally even laughed. Eventually, everyone piled into their cars and went home. They drove north or south or to the airport, but I remained. Somewhere just a few miles away, her family was gathered in much the same way. People would leave, and others would stay, but she was forever missing at our tables.

I went back to the same church that night. I volunteer with youth, and though I'd been given a pass for the evening, I wanted to go. I wanted to sing in the same place I had mourned. Where I still mourn. I pulled into the same parking lot I'd fled only hours earlier, but the whole campus had shifted in that short time span. The portraits and personal effects had come down, and Christmas decorations had started to come out. I wondered if they had waited. A nod to our grief, clearing out the programs and photos before setting up for joy and expectancy.

It caught me by surprise. Of course, loss happens all the time. Even amid celebratory seasons. Death has always given way to life. In no way did I feel rushed in my sadness; this dark cloak is still the only thing that seems to make sense. Instead, I felt like the curtain had been pulled back a bit. A reminder that many are carrying their hard things into this season too.

Hope. Peace. Joy. Love: Advent could not come fast enough, and the order has never made more sense to me. I wondered if this season could somehow have both. Mourning and celebration. If this building could hold both only hours apart, maybe so could I.

I climbed the stairs and saw several faces I had seen earlier in the day. I had shed my funeral clothes, but not my grief. I sang. I hugged. I was present, and I was completely somewhere else. My whole life I have been jealous of people who had a certainty or a faith that I just never seemed to hold. Instead, in this moment, my loose faith finally felt like it fit. One that expects questions and can hold anger and has space to let

other people's prayers and songs take the place of my own for a while. A faith that is indeed big enough even in its smallness.

It has been a few weeks. My concentration and sleep are finally returning. The hard feelings softening a bit. Grief can still occasionally surprise me and take my breath away, but mostly life keeps going. The dishes get put away and the emails answered. I question the old adage that time heals all wounds; instead I'd argue that time just etches us with scars.

Either way, time does indeed march onward. It is the season for soccer games, dinners, concerts and parties. My calendar is full even if my heart is heavy, and I find myself pulling into my driveway long after dark many nights. Each night I notice more holiday lights up in the neighborhood. A welcome brightness. I let my daughter play Christmas songs and we take extra laps around the block. I say she needs to practice driving, but mostly I need the light. At work, we share the best neighborhoods and addresses for decorated homes around town. The whole world has lit up when I have felt the darkest. And I am glad for all this extra light. I need every tiny bulb and bit of brightness I can find.

Not long ago, someone patiently talked to me about a friend she'd lost much longer ago. A mentor, taken from her. She found herself doing some of the impossible things that I am doing. Everything in her lit up as she remembered. She was there, but she was somewhere else. Her eyebrows lifted. Her eyes smiled, and all the energy in the room shifted. Everything in her got brighter.

Since my friend died, everything in me has felt dimmer. I'm not there yet.

But it offers a hope that one day I will be. A hope that one day, when I talk about my lost friend, my eyes won't flood and my heart won't clamp shut. No one will need to remind me to breathe, but instead I will remember, and I will light up. My eyes will twinkle like Christmas lights.

I look at the holiday lights with hope and I hold on to the darkness just a little bit longer. I am finding room for both. Christmas lights aren't exciting during the day. You can see them, but they aren't impressive. You can't coordinate them to music or have them dance across the lawn in the fullness of day. The show only starts after the sun sets. The darkness itself isn't bad, though it is heavy and fearful and makes it hard to see the way forward. Sometimes it is necessary. In the case of Christmas lights, it is the darkness that lets them shine so brightly.

I wish that weren't true.

But it is a truth I need right now.

This darkness will somehow make the light more beautiful if I let it.

My favorite part of Christmas Eve service is where they turn out all the lights.

When it gets dark and hushed and holy. And we sing a quiet song instead of a joyful one. The light is passed person to person. Slowly. Inefficiently. With care not to drip wax or put the tiny flame out. And eventually the whole place is lit up. But not the usual light; these bits of brightness come from each other. Flames flickering. Casting shadows. When we find each other in the dark, it creates a warmth and a glow that you don't get from the usual overhead lighting.

Finally, everyone is invited to hold up their light and something feels empowering about that. This tiny stick of fire held over our heads, doing its best to not let the darkness put it out.

It is a holy and beautiful feeling that I look forward to all season.

But it doesn't happen without darkness.

If you hold up your candle and sing all the way to the last verse,

It is its own dawn of redeeming grace.[38]

PART III
ORDINARY LOVE

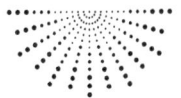

"The psalmist declares, 'This is the day that the Lord has made.' This one. We wake not to a vague or general mercy from a far-off God. God, in delight and wisdom, has made, named, and blessed this average day. What I in my weakness see as another monotonous day in a string of days, God has given as a singular gift."—— **Tish Harrison Warren**, *Liturgy of the Ordinary: Sacred Practices in Everyday Life*

40 LOVE

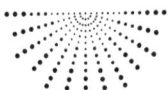

I WOULD LIKE TO THINK THAT I AM CONTENT WITH MY kids being their own people.

That I'm proud that they have their own interests and dreams that very rarely line up with mine, or the ones I imagined for them.

Of course my teenagers did not like things I liked. They often quit the ones that I liked for them, and I even let them. I want desperately to love my kids for who they are and not who I want them to be. I'm desperate to not press my own faults and preferences on them.

I can't even begin to describe the gush and warmth I feel when I look at baby pictures or cheer them on for something amazing they are doing. It is a love that is big and huge and all-consuming. And yet, occasionally, I see my own faults and my ordinariness in them and wince. I see lack of effort, motivation and ambition and want to light their fire. I see anxiety and fear stopping them from something they want. They are the best of me and the worst of me and something entirely new. They are people I know the best and occasionally not at all. I love them fiercely, but sometimes I love who I want them to be more...even though I think who they really are is by far the most beautiful.

I look at myself more often from that lens, so unsatisfied. Always thinking I should be more. And I want like hell to look at the people I love and be content with exactly who they are.

When I am most honest, I'm not sure that I do.

I want more for them too. But it is a fine line.

To want more for them because we love them, and loving them but wanting them to be more.

As a teenager, I had a terrible perception of who I was.

If you asked me then, I'd claim to be miserably average.

I didn't think I had much going for me.

I didn't think my teachers, family, boys, noticed me.

I thought that I was forgettable. Ordinary.

I wasn't comfortable in my body. I thought that there was nothing special about me.

I felt alone and unnoticed.

Now, a lot of years and a little bit of therapy later, the evidence doesn't match.

I graduated near the top of my class. I still have some of the friends I made when I was that age — but more importantly, I learned the skills to build meaningful relationships now.

I won all kinds of awards and accolades for music. I was a Varsity athlete. I'm all over my high school yearbook. I've been to high school reunions, and my old teachers and classmates didn't just remember me — they wanted to know the me-now. I'd love to fit back into my high school jeans, but more than skinny jeans I wish that I'd seen the evidence. Back then I didn't feel seen. There were legitimate reasons for that, but the loss is that I didn't even accurately see myself.

Not feeling seen meant that I struggled to see myself how God saw and loved me.

I have always understood that God loves me collectively. I mean

She loves everyone, right? However, because I didn't feel seen individually, I had a harder time understanding that God loved me individually. I didn't connect a loving God to a personal one. A God who sees me, all of me, and loves me anyway — well, that lands differently.

I love a grand-gesture in movies. For example, I adore when Mark shows up at Juliet's door in *Love Actually* or Lloyd blasts Peter Gabriel through a boombox in *Say Anything*.

But the truth is that in real life I prefer the ordinary. I love when my husband does the dishes or my kids take in the groceries without being asked. I love nothing more than when a friend brings me a coffee or offers to share their fries. Showboating is great in the movies, but in my real life I just want people who are willing to show up. I want love that sits beside rather than holds up a stereo. To quote Jerry Maguire[38], I don't need the big, impassioned speech; "You had me at hello."

I have found that so many people appreciate the everydayness of love rather than the big grand gesture. We want to watch the romcom, but we want to live into the steady and hard. One is an escape, but the other is true. Sometimes we love the idea of a person or thing more than the reality of them. Sometimes we love who we want them to be instead of figuring out who they actually are.

I think most of us really want what is true, even if it scares us. We want to be seen and loved in the same way by our families, our friends and our God. I think for me it is the only hope for loving my whole self. I'm certain every self-help book would tell me that I have the order wrong. That I need to love myself before I can love others, but 1 John 4:19[41] tells me otherwise. "We love because He first loved us".

I had a friend read that verse at my wedding instead of the more popular 1 Corinthians passage. Back then, I still had no clue what I was promising, who I was or who my kids would be. Honestly, we are all four still figuring it out. I am loved, so I can love. I can love the faults and the ordinary and the truth. All my life I have wanted to love others well, even those who have loved me imperfectly. For me, loving well has not been the hard part. Instead, the lesson of my life has been learning that I am loved. A kind of love that looks both in the mirror and others and doesn't have to cringe or want for more. Not a love that completes us, instead a love that is made complete in us[40]. I've had the order wrong all along. The beginning was the end. The end was the beginning.

In tennis, a score of zero is called "love." Love is the beginning. Love is the baseline. And often love is the score when you lose. Love isn't a win or an ace. It is simply showing up and a willingness to try. I think I sometimes make the same mistake with my faith. I think that loving God requires big movie-style gestures, like a Mother Teresa style life to really love God. That surely I can't love Him with a tired prayer shot off at a red light or making the same mistakes over and over again. Thankfully, love is more like tennis than the movies.

Love is the baseline. It is the beginning. He loves us first. All of us, even the parts we can't see yet. God is love, and all I have to do is simply show up, no boombox or ace required.

DOORFRAMES

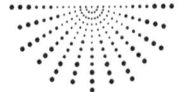

I SPENT ALMOST TWO DECADES TEACHING HIGH SCHOOL. Eventually, all the years started to blur together. My own days punctuated by six weeks, proms, graduations, and pep rallies. It was like living my own life on some kind of repeat. When people asked me what was new, it was easier to tell what was new with my kids than myself. They were constantly changing. Outgrowing their clothes, joining a soccer team, balancing equations, learning to read or playing the drums.

We lived in the same home from the time I brought them bundled from the hospital until my son turned eleven and my daughter eight. Every few months I'd take a sharpie and make them stand flat on their feet and mark their height next to their initials. For eleven years these black and red marks inched their way up the doorframe.

My next-door neighbor and I shared a pediatrician. I was surprised one day when she told me our doctor had suggested she see an endocrinologist. Her younger son already towered over mine. I asked her about it at our next checkup and she explained that she only refers someone when their growth is stalled, not when it is slow. She pulled up my son's growth charts to show me the gradual slope. "See" she said, "he is growing — just at his own rate." I can only hope that applies to adults as well. When my daughter reached that age, she'd occasionally wake up screaming in the middle of night. If it wasn't her ears or a nightmare, I'd rub her legs until she fell back asleep. Again, I asked the pediatrician if this was normal and she promised me that growing pains were real, but not to worry unless they became disruptive. She explained that it isn't the bones that hurt but the muscles being stretched. Her sharpie marks ticked up the same door frame.

I'm not overly sentimental. I didn't save every piece of my kids' art (I saved my favorites — I'm not a monster). I haven't held on to every outfit or stuffed animal, only a few. However, while packing up to move, I asked my husband if we could keep the door frame. He sighed, walked out to the garage and came back in with a crowbar. We moved on, but I brought the door frame with me. I couldn't bear to paint over it or leave it behind. I kept the evidence. Proof that they used to be small. Of who they were. But also, of what my pediatrician taught me. That growth can be gradual, and sometimes it will hurt enough to make you cry out in the night. That it stretches us to become more. I'm trying to figure out these parts of me, who I've been and how I've grown. I need those same lessons. I'm not sure how to mark it. I want my own proof.

My favorite part of my job is professional learning, but a good amount of my time is spent measuring growth, ensuring average yearly progress. We test the hell out of kids. I hate it, but one of the things I appreciate is a shift away from average scores and more towards growth. Most states have adjusted how they grade districts to factor this in. After each round of benchmarks or standardized tests, I'm required to crunch the data, to show any gains (or losses) from the previous years. I am constantly measuring and color-coding growth. A few weeks ago, I had my mid-year review. My boss went down the list and checked off everything in the highest column. We talked through the criteria, and much as I mostly want to hear I'm doing a great job, I stopped before signing it and said she needed to give me something to work on. She hesitated for a second, and I offered a place where I could use some work. She helped me set some goals. I wanted my own evidence for what I was doing right and where I needed to re-focus or stretch. Still, all these years later, I'm seeking sharpie marks.

I'm generally good at setting goals and taking incremental steps to reach them. I thrive on accountability and am not above making my own sticker chart or celebrating the smallest of wins with pie. My daughter would call me a "try-hard," and that is somehow not a compliment. I'm driven, but I'm not type A. It often confuses people, but maybe it is that I care way more about growth than I do success. I want to do better and be better but don't care all that much about being the best. I need to see progress to feel motivated enough to keep going. And that is the rub.

For several years, I've been working with a therapist. I've been unpacking my past and my hang ups. Like most hard things, sometimes I start off feeling worse instead of better and I finally realized this is because I don't know how to measure internal growth. Progress here is hard to name. I don't think this kind of work is linear; I think it comes in layers, and I feel frustrated each time I find myself coming back around to the same spot.

There are no green bar graphs or performance reviews. There is no such thing as adequate yearly progress for my heart. Occasionally I've set some goals, but they mostly shift and change before I can set the next right step. I know that it helps to keep showing up, and that sometimes it feels like being ripped open. I feel the shifts even if I can't name them. Even if sometimes they are so small. I know that I feel safer and steadier and softer. Mostly, I just feel more of everything.

I think sometimes I'd like for the kind and patient woman across from me to just tell me where I've grown and what I should be working on, but I know that it is best if I do the work. I'm tired of doing the work, except *I am the work*. There is an E.E. Cummings quote I love, "it takes courage to grow up and become who you really are.[42]"

I feel like this is what I'm trying so hard to do. It takes courage and a million layers and ache. I want there to be a finish line, a finality to who I am. Except that sounds a lot like death. I'd rather grow. And ache. And rest. And celebrate and do it all over again. Layer after layer. Inch after inch. Shift after shift. I wonder if Cummings should have written, "to grow up and become who you really are and were." That maybe this is all an undoing as much as it is a becoming. At least it is for me.

My kids are now teenagers. I don't really mark doorframes anymore. We did it a few times in our new home, but mostly that season has passed. I asked, years after we moved in and filled all the closets and garages with too many things, where the doorframe ended up. My husband found it in the garage, and I brought it inside. It was just a dusty piece of broken wood covered in sharpies, initials and dates. But is also evidence of growth.

I moved it into the corner of my home office. I smile when I lean back and see it. But I want the same evidence and reminder for myself. So I go into the garage (which might as well be half of a Lowes store) and find a long thin piece of wood. I get a sharpie. I start with moving away from home and I inch my way up. I mark progress with single words and events. I read back over some of my emails and essays. Some years are lost, but there are enough. I mark it over and over again. I leave plenty of room at the top for things I haven't learned yet. I place my own evidence into the same corner of my office next to my rescued door frame.

I must have assumed that my kids growing up would only be about them — their progress and experiences, but in many ways it has also been about mine. Surely, I have grown as much as they have. Maybe more. Like their pediatrician reminded me, growth can be gradual and sometimes it will hurt. And all of it counts.

HOME (THIS IS TWENTY)

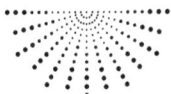

I WAS A MESS AT NINETEEN. I KNEW WHO I (THOUGHT) I wanted to be, I just didn't have the discipline to get there. I did very few things whole-heartedly. I skipped class. I semi-committed. I could never remember to rinse out my cereal bowl (OK, I still struggle with that.) I worked out, but then ate my weight in chips and salsa. I changed my hair color about as often as I changed my sheets. I got tiny tattoos that I thought I could hide. I changed my major. I didn't make many good decisions when I was nineteen, but I did make at least one. I said yes when a shaggy-haired guy who desperately needed to shave asked me to a soccer game. He forgot to ask for my number or say how we'd get to this soccer game. But it was enough.

From the beginning, it felt different. Mostly I just tried not to screw it up (and I did a few times). We were both nineteen. And had no idea who we were. We thought we were grownups.

But we were babies barely old enough to vote. Our hardest decisions were what to eat, whether to study or watch a movie. But I knew he was home. That is the only word that has ever described him. I've been a "we" longer than I've been a "me."

At nineteen, I wasn't quite ready to settle down, but three years later he asked me to marry him anyway. In a proposal that was a little awkward and confusing. And maybe that is only fitting. We were twenty-three when we got married. This time we really thought we were grown.

I had an actual teaching job with health insurance and dry cleaning.

He had a job offer in Arlington. But we were babies barely old enough to drink the champagne at our wedding (and there was lots of champagne).

I packed a U-haul and moved east. Home.

We promised all the things that are written in traditional marriage vows. I think my twenty-three-year-old self heard all the good things. To have and to hold, for better, for richer, in health. And those things are true. But at forty-three, and hopefully at eighty-three, I cherish the other halves to those promises more. Forever feels different to a nineteen-year-old. Or a twenty-three-year-old. It feels like honeymoon forever. Wedding gifts to unpack, thank-you cards to write and airplanes to catch. Warm feelings filling your chest. Adventures. "From this day forward" feels way less romantic than "forever." From this day forward is more like hitting the snooze button, or morning breath or lost keys or soccer games or who is going to take off because one of the kids is sick. Again.

But here is what it also means. Moving forward together. Big decisions and emergency rooms and funerals. Celebrations and budgets and first days and last days and a million in between. It means choosing you over and over and over again.

For worse. No one gets to see your faults like people you live with. Ask anyone with a teenager. Or in a marriage. Sometimes you save your worst for the people you love the most. It isn't fair. But it is because you are secure. You are loved. Even at your worst. Even if I will have to apologize later.

For poorer. In college, poorer meant I had to go to the used CD place and sell music so we could eat out. As an adult, it means I've had to borrow money from my elementary-age son. Or ask for a loan when my child has some medical expenses I can't cover. It means watching the bank account balance dwindle. It means not getting the things I want. It means making financial decisions that aren't just about you. He is the saver. I'm the spender. There have been plenty of fights over money. And even when our bank account didn't show it, we have always felt lucky with all that we have been given.

In sickness. It means dropping your husband off at the ER. It means multiple COVID swabs. It means food poisoning on your honeymoon. It means getting older. It means copays and fighting with the insurance. It means living wills and ICUs. It means someone being there when they are wheeled off and when you wake up. Sickness is scary and vulnerable. And marriage means there is a hand to hold and someone to help fight the insurance company with.

We bought a puppy. And then a house. We cashed in some old stocks and traveled.

We had a baby.

And then another.

We fought and we danced and we wept and we watched TV.

We made hard decisions and easy ones.

We feasted and we overdrew our accounts.

We painted and mowed the lawn and took out the trash.

Five years turned into ten and now into twenty.

We made a home. And my handy husband built many of the things inside it.

Like bookshelves and places to hang out keys so we aren't forever losing them.

But he also built a supportive place to become that person my nineteen-year-old self would be proud of.

We are no longer babies. Our babies are no longer babies. One of them can drive.

Our hair is starting to gray. My husband's hair is no longer shaggy, but our son's is.

We have gained weight. And lost it. And gained it again. (repeat for the rest of our lives).

Some days we mostly talk logistics — who has what practice when.

Some days I go to sleep early (most days for me).

I have read thousands of books. He has spent that many hours in the garage.

But some days we laugh or encourage or go for a walk together.

We fight. We make up. We forget to put out the trash. But we do it together.

Twenty years feels like forever and a moment.

We are completely different people than we were at nineteen. We have grown and learned and read and experienced so much more life. Our faith has changed; we have new hobbies. Our musical tastes have shifted, our palates have adjusted. Our titles, priorities and our blood pressure — all new. Some better. Some worse. But we have navigated those changes together. Sometimes sloppy and awkward. Sometimes with grace. Sometimes with yelling.

Our marriage is literally older than we were when we met.

It is the only home I want.

Being married to someone for twenty years means I know things I didn't know at nineteen.

I know that he smells of hair gel, deodorant and sawdust.

I know his cough three aisles away in the grocery store.

I know that when he says he is going to the store, that he means Lowes and not Kroger.

I know that when we fight, we mostly just need time.

That we will make up. That we will try again. I know that he will be there when it matters.

That we will always be home.

LAST

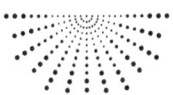

No one would ever mistake me for a dance mom. I can barely tell the difference between a leotard and a swimsuit. My girl has been in dance for over four years, and I'd still rather vacuum than help her put wiggle into tights — which is really saying a lot. Her debut was a Junior League Christmas shopping event where they had squeezed a stage in the corner and invited local dance studios to perform while women shopped for all things Santa and rhinestones.

My daughter was barely out of pull ups. I realize this is awfully young for organized classes of any kind, but after much pressure from anyone who watched her shake and twirl anywhere music was playing, I relented.

After dozens of unsolicited performances in the grocery store checkout, between tables at restaurants and even in the aisle at church, I bought the tiniest of ballet slippers and the most annoying tap shoes and signed her up. Her class only had a few members, and while lining up for her Christmas debut, I learned that one girl in her class was sick, and the other had had a death in the family. That was it. Her class had three members, and quickly her trio had fallen to a solo act. I wondered what she would do when she walked out on the now seemingly huge stage and realized she was alone. I feared how she would respond in front of all these people when the music started.

I decided that if she panicked or froze I would climb up there with her and go through the motions. Even at three, my daughter's dancing skills had already surpassed my own, and I assure you this would be entertaining for all, but not for the right reasons. Instead, my girl got up there, her eyes huge as she looked nervously into the crowd. The music began and she absolutely nailed it. She did not need rescuing, and I gave that girl a standing ovation.

My daughter is older now, and I think this is her last season to dance. I don't weep at recitals anymore (except maybe because they are so long). Today, as I walked out of her elementary school, I felt the same way as when I first saw her alone on a stage. My heart in my stomach. Love and pride bursting me wide open. Her school hosts an oratorical contest and every year a single student is chosen from each class to compete. These students recite their memorized poem in front of the entire school, a bunch of parents and the most scary: a panel of serious-looking judges. For the last three years in a row, I have found my seat in the back of the cafeteria. First for my son and the last two years for my daughter.

My son is quiet and shy, and so I was surprised that he was chosen. I asked him to practice and he wouldn't even read his poem to me, but he got on the stage and said it in front of hundreds of people. Again, my heart swelled and nearly broke me open. He took last place.

The next year my daughter, only a kindergartener, was asked to compete. She shook a little and rushed her poem, but the thought of a grown up me speaking in front of that many people makes my knees wobble. Like her brother, she took last place.

She competed again today. She repeated her poem quietly but with a little more confidence and inflection. She took third place.

Third may sound impressive, but the truth is that it was next-to-last place. Still, I felt that same ridiculous pride as I walked back to my car.

It felt just like every time my son stood at bat and I prayed he didn't strike out. Every time they spoke at a school play and I secretly hoped they wouldn't forget the lines. How I feel every time my son runs across a finish line in a race. How I felt when he gave a speech in a library full of parents as Ross Perot. He kept talking even when his fake ear started to slide down the side of his head.

They are older; they have changed so much and so quickly, but my heart feels the exact same. Just like the Elizabeth Stone quote[43] on having a child: "It is to decide forever to have your heart go walking around outside your body."

It will soon be awards season at the schools my children attend. I will rush over between classes. Hug them and tell them I am proud of them. I will take a picture of each one with their certificate. But the truth is, my heart doesn't feel the same rush. It doesn't want to bust as each kid, mine included, receives a certificate. Getting an award just for participating, doesn't quite feel significant.

I am most proud of my kids when they do hard, scary things. Things that require work, kindness, or knocking knees. When they have the opportunity to fail. When they are brave, despite a panel of judges or roomful of peers or suddenly no one. In ballet slippers, soccer cleats or church shoes.

Rarely do kids get awards for being brave. These days most awards are handed out for performance or participation. Competing at something that you are good at is not nearly as scary as showing up when you feel ordinary, as dancing alone rather than with the crowd. Sometimes the best kind of trophies or certificates look more like last place than first.

QUARTERS

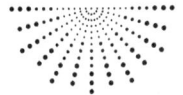

I'VE REACHED THE AGE WHERE MY IDEAL FRIDAY NIGHT involves pajamas, a couch, a book and being asleep by ten o'clock. (ok, 9:30). The twenty- to thirty-year-old version of me had a very different idea of an ideal Friday night. At twenty, I'd hope for a date, a bar or a large group of friends. At thirty, I still hoped for an invite of some kind. A dinner party or excuse to wear anything besides yoga pants or school clothes. I wanted to be included and invited and to laugh the loudest. Don't get me wrong; I still want to be invited, but I don't always want to go.

My life seemed to narrow in the last decade. Even before our season of the forced-isolation pandemic, I found myself skipping events, not always responding to texts and working to strengthen my circle of friends rather than just grow it. I started to choose depth over width and have never regretted it. One of my favorite childhood friends, Laura, has a saying (well, it actually came from Al Capone[44]): "Be careful who you call your friends. I'd rather have four quarters than a hundred pennies."

I'm always friend-shopping, but as I get older, I find I'm significantly more choosy about the people to whom I want to give my time and my stories. Quarters are bigger and worth more than all the pennies. Over the years, I've seen my friend list decrease in size but increase in value. As I've hit hard times in my life, that couldn't be truer. My circles have shrunk. The pennies have gotten lost and slipped through the cracks, but the value of my quarter friends has only grown.

Friendships are easy when we are young. We stumble into them. I made my first best friend in second grade. I'd just moved to a new school, and we met on the playground. We had the same chili-bowl haircut, but that might be where our commonalities ended.

As we age, friendships are both harder to make and to keep. They are work, yet we want them to be easy. It often takes a scheduling miracle to have dinner. I love getting to know new people and will never consider my dance card full, but maintaining friendships is work. It is an investment of time when I'd rather be on my couch. It is returning texts when I just want to respond later (which will turn into never). It is going first and sometimes second. It is saying you are sorry. It is letting that little stuff go. Quarters invest and apologize.

I'm not the easiest person to be friends with. I talk more than I listen. I speak before I think. I'm not always sensitive to the same things my friends are. I don't mind a debate. I take up more space than I offer. I'm not the best secret keeper. I struggle to cut my losses. I have strong opinions. The quarters in my life are not perfect either, but what they do perfectly is show up when it matters. They are there to cheer me on and to ache with me. Quarters call you out on the hard stuff and fill you up when you are empty. I don't need a hundred people to do this, only a few.

The other day a coworker was encouraging a friend whose son was going through a rough time at school. She told her, "All he needs is just one good friend." One friend will make all the difference. One quarter.

My own kids have yet to find their best friend. I tell them, "Don't worry, I didn't meet some of mine until my twenties." I'm still finding them in my forties. I pray for a friend like that for them, but unlike my coworker, I don't ask for just one. I pray that they find a few quarters. I pray they have a generous, kind friend who is up for almost anything. I pray they have a loyal friend who may not always answer her phone but can always be counted on when it matters. I pray they have people to go on adventures with, and laugh with, but mostly that they have a place where they feel most themselves. A few people who they invest in and value are worth far more than a hundred pennies. A few quarters are gold.

MINE: A TRIBUTE.

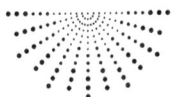

For almost a month in July, they were mine. A few dozen fifteen and sixteen-year-old girls.

They came from some of the best neighborhoods and private schools to group homes and everything in between. And somehow, magically, the guards and labels and cars and boyfriends and social status didn't seem to make it very far past those slamming double screen doors.

It only took a few nights on those hard bunks, hearing each other snore and cry and fart and giggle, for everyone to start getting real. No one put on their makeup in the morning. Hair air-dried or immediately went up into a ponytail, and the closet was a big community one.

During the day we swam, fished, crafted, walked up a lot of hills and stole ice from the ice machines. After lunch they read the newest Harry Potter books on their bunks and passed around the latest *Seventeen* magazine. Or shaved their legs with spray bottles. Dug through their caboodles. Listened to their Discmans. Wrote their friends or boys and occasionally even their parents. And later we would dance in the alcove, run people's bras up the flagpole, sneak forbidden snacks and wonder what the night's activity would be.

Late at night, those bunks were always at least two-deep. And it didn't matter if we were sticking to plastic mattress covers or lying flat on our backs on the tennis courts, looking at the stars: two hours into our scheduled fifteen-minute devotional or singing around a campfire, their stories spilled out.

And some of the stories were really normal.

They weren't pretty enough.

Or popular enough.

They missed home.

Or their parents were splitting up.

They were jealous.

Or they'd never even kissed a boy.

Or they'd given their last boyfriend too much of themselves.

And some of them broke my heart.

They threw up after every meal.

They were abused and berated.

Their dad was in jail.

Their mom had taken off.

Their parents were addicted.

They were addicted.

They were deep in depression and had contemplated suicide.

I don't know if I ever said the right words.

But I listened. And I lay there.

And I told my own stories and insecurities.

And I snuck a few of them out to check email or raid the fridge or walk across the catwalk late at night. To keep having those conversations. Because I didn't know how to heal broken hearts, but I knew how to be present.

. . .

AT THE END of those long, hot weeks, I was spent. And drained. And emotionally exhausted.

I had given them every single piece of me. I was tired and sunburned and out of clean clothes. And I was completely empty, and so ready to get home. But I knew it mattered. I knew it was important. Because once someone had done it for me. When I had slept and written my name in sharpie on those exact same bunks. In the exact same alcove. Spilling out my own stories and hoping for someone to listen. She did, and it changed me. And I knew that it was my turn to do the same.

I had taught some of them how to put in a tampon, and bait their hooks, make a banana boat, how to do a jump serve, how to pray, that doing a belly flop off the dam is a really bad idea, how to tip a canoe, to expect retaliation if they came after me with water balloons, how to hit a bull's eye, what I think God sounds like, how to properly wrap a bunk with toilet paper, and how to get their sheets to stop slipping off those miserable mattresses.

And they taught me how to love with my whole heart until it was so empty that it was full.

AT THE END OF JULY, they all went home. Back to their fancy neighborhoods and group homes and happy families and complicated ones that I didn't want to think about. I started teaching high school. I got married the next summer instead of reclaiming my bunk. The good one by the fire escape and a decent breeze. Back then, there was no social media to make keeping up easy, but a few of us managed. I got letters and emails and mix tapes in the mail. We caught up over pizza and coffee and ice cream when we happened to be in the same town. There was a whole table of these girls at my wedding. I've been to more than a few of theirs.

These girls aren't girls anymore. They are grown. And wives and mothers and girlfriends.

Some of them are doctors and lawyers and most of them have real grownup jobs and health insurance. Some of them live across the country and some of them have traveled places I've only read about. At least one of them lives in my own town. No matter their age or zip code, they are still mine.

To be honest, for the most part, I've lost touch with most of them. Life kind of does that.

Even with social media. But this morning I was logging onto my computer and I saw on a Facebook post that one of them had just had a baby. I proceeded to do what you always do on social media when someone has a birthday or a baby or says something funny or is going through something hard. I started to post on her wall, but suddenly that didn't feel like enough. Immediately, I flashed back to this girl with short hair and sassy at fourteen, giving me a run for my money in the intermediate dorm; and later at sixteen, beautiful, fierce. And I remembered all the stories she'd told on those bunks. And the hard that she had lived. Just a few years earlier, I remembered tears quietly slipping down my face as she walked down the aisle. And my son dancing at her reception. I knew right then that posting my congratulations wasn't going to cut it. She is the one that lives in my town, but I didn't know her number or even the hospital. That didn't stop me from literally sprinting out the door. Without brushing my hair or brushing my teeth. Just like one of those July mornings because suddenly I couldn't get there fast enough. I drove too fast and called hospitals on the way. And got it on the first try.

Room 207.

I suspect her camp counselor was the last girl she was expecting to walk in the room.

But her still face lit up when I did, and I almost crawled straight into her hospital bed with her because it would have been just like one of those bunks. Instead, I went immediately to hold her beautiful baby girl, named after her grandmother. The exact same one that used to send her to camp every summer. I pulled up a chair and let her tell me a few more stories. Because in some of the most important ways, she is still part of mine.

Kathleen Bridges England. March 16, 1985 - November 7, 2023.

GEESE AND BELONGING

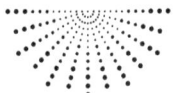

Recently, on vacation, my husband asked what a group of turkeys is called? My son, a walking nature documentary, had to look it up. "A rafter" he shared, but then went down the rabbit hole for groups of animals, and we even made up a few of our own. (By the way, a group of rabbits is called a fluffle, which is adorable). There can be a battery of barracudas, a murder of crows, a destruction of wild cats, a flamboyance of flamingos, a tower of giraffes, a skulk of foxes or a conspiracy of lemurs. Some group names even depend on what they are doing — for example, vultures in flight are called a kettle, when feeding they are called a wake and just resting in a tree is called a committee (which makes me understand how things in committee often get so little done).

The day before on a hike, he'd gone all nature documentary (again) to tell us that a group of Aspen trees is really considered a singular organism. And there is some debate on whether a group of aspens is the world's biggest organism (not a killer whale or a redwood) or a community of interconnected trees. A group in this case called a quake. I try to argue with him, tell him that individually these trees could survive, so I'm not sure I buy the whole singular organism bit. Of course, he knows far more about this than I do, and tells me about their interconnected root systems and dependence on one other. Even trees can't live without community.

Regardless of what you call it, there are names for belonging across the kingdoms. Maybe it is just us humans that struggle with it.

IF YOU SEARCH THE WORD "BELONGING" on the internet long enough, you will eventually land on some Mary Oliver because maybe there are some places that only poets can take us.

I know my Mary. I sometimes worry about what I am doing with my "one wild and precious life.[45]" I try to remember that a "box full of darkness[46]" too can be a gift. When I write, I do my best to follow her instructions: to pay attention, to be astonished and to tell about it.[47] And it's even harder to follow her advice on how to live in this world: "To love what is mortal, to hold them and then when it is time to let them go.[48]"

For belonging, it is a poem about geese that always comes up:[49]

You do not have to be good.
 You do not have to walk on your knees
 for a hundred miles through the desert, repenting.
 You only have to let the soft animal of your body
 love what it loves.
 Tell me about despair, yours, and I will tell you mine.
 Meanwhile the world goes on.
 Meanwhile the sun and the clear pebbles of the rain
 are moving across the landscapes,
 over the prairies and the deep trees,
 the mountains and the rivers.
 Meanwhile the wild geese, high in the clean blue air,
 are heading home again.

Whoever you are, no matter how lonely,
the world offers itself to your imagination,
calls to you like the wild geese, harsh and exciting—
over and over announcing your place
in the family of things.

ODDLY ENOUGH, it never mentions belonging by name. It starts by telling us what belonging is not. Being good. Walking on our knees. Leaving ourselves. The rest of the poem provides the instructions on how to belong instead of fit in: share our hard parts. Love what you love. Soften. And like the wild geese, find your place in the "family of things."

What Mary doesn't tell us but most of us can picture is that geese always fly in a V-shape. A recognizable pattern that nature websites[50] (and my son) explains is primarily to conserve energy. Flying in a uniform shape allows each goose to draft off the one in front of it. They take turns being in front and providing a wind break. The shape is also supposed to make it easy to keep up with everyone in the group.

Belonging isn't forcing ourselves into places we might not fit, but over and over announcing your place "in the family of things." We are asked to name our spaces and our people. Over and over, in case it changes or in case we do. We are born into families, but we can also choose them. We get a new name in the community, like vultures, based on our context.

We can be coworkers or friends or a team or a mob. We can travel together to conserve energy, or we can exhaust ourselves on our own. Meanwhile the world goes on whether you are a goose or a person. Whether you are lonely or can name your place. A group of geese, by the way, is called a gaggle.

When I give myself names that belong to a group instead of just my own, my priorities change. My world gets bigger. I used to think that belonging was being chosen, but maybe belonging is more about choosing to put myself in the context of others — my friends, my community, my family. Belonging is less about knowing your place and more about finding it. Belonging gives us permission to make our own family of things, and call it whatever we want.

A gaggle or a quake or a murder or a coalition or a bloat or a zeal or a skulk.

Or loved. Or wanted. Or safe. Or seen. Or valued.

GIFTS OF ASKING AND GOING SECOND

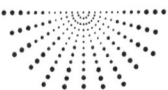

Going Second

IN COLLEGE, the big thing was accountability groups or prayer groups. I always left feeling terrible, like I was doing something wrong and I was just not made right. That something in me was broken because I couldn't pull it together like everyone else.

But the truth was, most everyone else was just lying. Either out loud or to themselves. Because they would ask for prayer for their sick grandmas. Or that they missed a quiet time. Or they only spent one hour in prayer that day instead of two.

When I shared, I spoke about the party I had been to the night before. Or my boyfriend that I needed to break up with but couldn't. Or the fact that I hadn't had a quiet time all week. And why doesn't the Bible mention the word "quiet time" if it is so important anyway? And when I had questions, I asked them. Even if they were ones I already knew the Sunday School answers to. I wanted to know how my friends went from knowing the right answer to actually feeling it. I was always met with a lot of stares.

Occasionally, people would write down verses for me to read or memorize. I'm sure they all remembered to pray for me, though I always lost the little notecard on which I wrote everyone else's requests. Eventually, I learned that some of those same people were struggling with some of the same things I was. Or even harder things. They just chose safer things to say out loud.

In the grownup world, I've found that only some of that has changed. I almost never sit around in accountability or prayer groups. Often we go around in Sunday school and voice concerns. They are rarely personal. But very occasionally, someone's voice cracks and tears slip out and they get real. Suddenly, the whole room changes. It softens and becomes more tender because one person was brave enough or desperate enough to show their need and their heart.

Someone always has to go first. Anne Jackson's *Permission to Speak Freely*[51] calls this the giving the gift of letting someone else go second. I've hung on to that phrase ever since.

When I fight with my husband, one of us has to apologize before the other. When I make a new friend, someone has to be the first to ask or tell or hug or show another layer. I used to spend a lot of time waiting, being second or third or fourth. Or sometimes never taking a turn at all. Because I didn't want to look dumb or be vulnerable or get hurt. Often going first backfires. because no one goes second. There is a shift in thinking about it as a gift that makes it easier. Over time I've also learned what I can give while still being careful with my heart. You can go first without giving it all away. That is the gift I've learned to give myself.

Ever since, I have done some things out of character. I've written kind emails. I've hit send. Or publish. Or apologized. Told my story. Or stammered through some awkward conversations. I've hugged and said I love you and asked people I want to be friends with if they want to get coffee. All when I didn't know how they'd respond. Occasionally, I heard no. Or nothing. Or didn't get a response at all. But more often than not, someone went second.

And it was a gift to both of us.

Asking

Ever had forty-three things on your to-do list and read or filled out one of those silly social media questionnaires? Checking off books you've read, movies you've watched, states you have visited, favorite breakfast cereal?

Me neither. Except I have. I am a sucker for them. I almost never share them; I just read and answer. I have taken almost every personality test out there. (Enneagram 7 here w/ a strong 8 wing, ENFJ). I read somewhere that people take personality tests, even the bad ones, in hopes of learning something new about themselves. We are all trying to figure out who we are...and maybe we will get closer if someone just asks us the right question. I'm not sure the answer to my being is in a quiz telling me what percentage of Betty White I am, but I still very much want to know. (The answer - 100%).

One of my least favorite things about therapy is when we get past the small talk and she just looks at me and waits. I know it is my turn to bring up the work. I'm a good student. I have prepared a list in my head of things I want to talk about and/or work on, but sometimes I still hesitate. I would rather she just ask me a question. I know what I want to say. I am paying for this time, but at the moment I'd still rather answer a question than just tell.

There is something easier about answering than telling.

I have a friend who hosts what she calls a veritable feast in her bookshop once a month. She brings in food and she reads passages from a few books, and you talk through a few simple questions or prompts at your table. That is it. That is the whole format. Good food, a short reading and intentional conversation, mostly with strangers. It is like a book club without having to read a book first. Also, the story you find yourselves talking about is yours and your new friends' more than any characters'. Each time I've walked away with new perspectives, insights, compassion and new questions rattling around in my head. You don't need to go to a feast for this — simply have a few prompts and a few people.

My favorite part from graduate school was that it gave me the opportunity to interview people. I sent emails to the smartest people I knew (and some that I didn't know) and asked if I could meet with them. Eventually, I had questions that were coded and used for research, but at first I just asked the things I wanted to know. What shocked me is that not a single person said no. Every person, even people way above my pay grade, made room on their busy schedules and answered my questions. Many seemed to enjoy it and a few even took their own notes. I learned that people generally like telling their story and sharing their expertise.

Most Sunday evenings, I help lead a group of high school girls at church. When I agreed to volunteer, I had anticipated serving a meal, subbing when someone was out or something simple. Instead, I found myself each week leading a dozen high school girls all talking at once around me. I have plenty of experience from my years in the classroom with teenagers, but getting them to talk still felt intimidating. It took me a few weeks to find my rhythm. The secret was simply asking questions (and showing up with good snacks). Sometimes they were the questions off the handout, but mostly they were things like:

How was your basketball game last week?

How is your grandmother?

Chick-fil-A or Canes?

Sometimes we have spent entire breakout sessions simply answering our high, low, buffaloes (high of the week, low point, and something random).

I have two teenagers of my own, and I know better to ask how school was. The answer is always, "Fine." What did you learn today? The answer is always, "Nothing." (Lies)

I've read the articles that have more specific suggestions:

What made you laugh today? Who did you sit with at lunch? Did you help anyone today?

It worked a little bit when they were younger, but now those still get me an eyeroll. My daughter will even occasionally ask if I read some article because a teenager loves to call you out. What they will do is answer outside questions. The more random the better. We used to get texts that had weekly questions to ask at dinner. Things like:

What is the weirdest dream you've ever had? If you could eat only one food for the rest of your life, what would it be? (Tacos, of course). If you joined the circus, what circus act would you be?

Those texts stopped showing up each Monday on my phone. I forgot about them, but my kids surprised me and asked what happened to the questions.

Sometimes I think we are afraid to share without the ask. I'm a pretty terrible listener. (I'm forever working on this), but I've always believed in the gift of going first (sharing, inviting, kindness), and now I am learning the value of the gift of asking. Questions are a springboard. A prompt or a question gives us an excuse to share. In most cases, we don't need an excuse, but somehow it feels less presumptuous than just telling. Asking is an easy way to show love. It is the gift that allows someone else to give themselves.

DIFFERENT

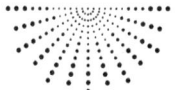

LIKE MOST GROWN ADULTS WITH EXCELLENT communication skills, I have entire text threads dedicated to memes. I'm in another group text that communicates almost exclusively through TikTok videos.

A friend sent a funny meme of a middle-aged woman covered in unflattering tattoos. This photo fell flat for me. I reminded her that I have over half a dozen tattoos myself (although none in such obvious places as in the picture). I thought about it while I washed my hair — and about how my hair was also once purple. I wondered what kind of memes could be found about people with bold hair choices or pierced noses. Other than the first two tattoos, I did none of these things in my youth. All were in my thirties.

Currently, my hair is a plain brown color, styled in a sensible cut. My tattoos are all easily hidden by most clothing, and only my ears are pierced. As this decade closes, I have made efforts to dress more professionally, drink less, stay on top of the laundry — although I still refuse to make my bed and talk at an appropriate volume level. Yet I only look back on my purple-haired days with longing rather than regret.

I used to do those things to be different. Sometimes I felt just a little trapped by my suburban life. Although perfect, it felt a little too predictable. I felt like I was going to lose myself in Starbucks cups, Target bags, and privilege. Other times, I just wanted to feel different. But I didn't know how, so I'd at least find a way to mark it. I'd mark it on my wrist or the top of my foot with a symbol to remind me. I'd go buy a box of just-a-tad-too-red hair dye and hope that looking different would be the same as feeling it.

In either case, I was no different than before...I just had some new ink or a bad dye job.

I'm glad for every permanent mark. I've learned that hair always grows back as you are, not who you want to be. Marks, be it tattoos or scars, always tell a story. This I know. I can't promise to never get another tattoo or always keep my hair close to my natural color, but I will tell you that I feel very differently about wanting to be different. I don't need to feel that way anymore.

People who want so desperately to be different never really have been.

When you actually are, all you want to feel is just like everyone else. At least that has been the case for me.

Years ago, I remember feeling isolated in so many ways. I had a new unusual health diagnosis and did not know anyone with the same condition. I could have really used a friend to sit down and have coffee with and ask a million questions. I hurt physically and emotionally in ways I never had before. All I wanted was for someone to relate. I felt different and isolated in the worst way because it was actually true: I was different.

In a way, my differences were easier than most because, for the most part, no one could spot them on the outside. No one could judge me for them. No one could kick me out of church or deny my rights. I found groups of people like me online. It is no cup of coffee or hug, but occasionally I have a forum where I can ask questions or just scroll through when I feel pain.

Growing up, there is such a tension between wanting to be different but not so different that we aren't like everyone else. Wanting to be you, but wanting to fit in. To still have a place. To still feel accepted and included.

Teenagers constantly walk in this tension. I guess I took a little longer to grow up than most. I don't mind. You have to be at least eighteen to get a tattoo anyway. And I probably needed to be at least thirty to be able to afford it. Not always, but for a long time now, I have made an effort to love people who are different than me. To include them. To march for them. To learn from them. I actually prefer it, and the more I listen, the more I realize how un-different we are.

I'm pretty boring and will use all the perspective I can get. Loving those that are different than me is still a skill I fall short in. I want so desperately to be different but am sometimes afraid of it. Afraid of what to say. Or do. Or doing it wrong. That it will rub off on me. Afraid that other people will judge me as different as well.

God, I hope they do.

Even if my hair is brown.

OSSOBUCO

I WOKE UP FROM SURGERY, MY THROAT SORE FROM THE ventilator, and I immediately reached to touch my face. I smiled. I gritted my teeth. I rubbed my nose. Gloriously, I felt nothing. Not the familiar electric shocks or burning sensations that ultimately led me to let someone cut a hole in my head and wrap my nerves in Teflon.

I thanked the doctor and felt giddy with relief, at least until the pain medicine started to wear off and my brain began to swell. The shocks returned as soon as I left ICU. Before they wheeled me out of the hospital, I had resigned myself to the fact that maybe the surgery did not work. Maybe I landed in the unlucky 15% that are not responsive to treatment. I came home with a shaved head, a new plate of metal screwed into my skull, and a defeated heart.

My parents came to visit and help after I was released. My pain level was off the chart. I'd get dizzy if I stood up for long. I couldn't read or watch TV. My mother worried and my dad went to the store. All he knew to do was cook. He spent hours in my kitchen. My knives and cookware were not up to his standards, so he went to the store and returned with the fanciest kitchen knife I have ever owned and a beautiful blue Le Creuset Dutch oven. It remains to this day the most expensive cooking item I own.

I slept away as much of the days as I could. I needed the lights and volume low and my speech was slow. My entire family had invested so much in me getting better that I felt like a disappointment, though I could not control the outcome. I'm not quite sure he understood the intensity of my surgery. He didn't know that I was barely clinging to hope. That I had run out of prayers. He chopped and stirred and comforted the best way he could. His prayers were tender and perfectly seasoned. I'm sure he felt helpless as to how to help; like the rest of us, he had hoped for healing, and instead all he had to offer was dinner. Others brought me a meal. My father cooked me a feast.

My husband gently woke me up to eat. My head spun walking the few dozen steps to the dining room, where I found the feast spread out on my hand-me-down kitchen table. Ossobuco, garlic potatoes, and crostini. A celebratory meal, in the time of my greatest disappointment. I have no idea where my father found the lamb, but it smelled warm and like love.

I did not have the appetite for anything in front of me, though it was one of my favorites. I had barely stomached more than Jello in the last few days. It took all my energy to get out of bed and sit upright in a chair.

The meal exhausted me, but it also restored me. My parents have always struggled to show me comfort, and I have since struggled to receive it. My father tried to heal and comfort me with a feast, and I did not want to disappoint. I ate more than I had in days. Not because I was hungry, but because I wanted to receive what he was trying to give.

Meals showed up at my door for at least a month following. Coworkers, neighbors, and friends all brought comfort foods — casseroles, enchiladas, and soups. Only my father served up veal shanks that he'd simmered all day. Others brought me a meal. My father cooked me a feast.

My hair grew back. The swelling went down. My nerves healed slowly but not completely. Sometimes a meal is more than a meal; even if you aren't hungry, it can still fill you up. It may not heal, but it can comfort.

Last night I cooked my family chili. I suppose any of the pots in my bottom cabinet would have done, but instead I used the blue Le Creuset that my father had left behind. Anything I make in that Dutch oven is a feast.

TASTE AND SEE

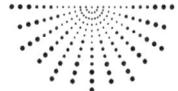

My daughter, like most teens, is conservative on the compliments about my parenting. Once she came home thanking me for not putting her in cotillion. I laughed and told her I did my time and would be happy to lend her my old Jessica McClintock dress and teach her the foxtrot. Both of those references were lost on her, but she was grateful all the same. Recently, she has thanked us for being a "food family". I didn't know there was such a thing, but I knew exactly what she meant as we ate the tiki masala I had made for dinner. The night before we'd ordered dumplings in chili oil and we talked about where I wanted to eat for my birthday. She has not always been an adventurous eater. She was extremely picky as a child — mostly sticking to chicken nuggets and cheese puffs. I had a friend at the time (a decade ahead of me in the child raising game) that told me not to fight my kids over food. To not force it, and that she'd come around eventually. I did my best to teach her to be polite (especially when she was with someone else) and just to say "no thank you" when she didn't want something. My in-laws once insisted she eat her green beans and she responded by puking out of sheer defiance.

She's still not a fan of green beans, but not only did she become a more adventurous eater, she is occasionally a pretentious one. One day my twelve-year-old daughter texted me while I was at work asking where we kept the white wine. I figured this deserved a return phone call. Recently my father had ordered a large bowl of steamed mussels for us and we devoured them, and then spent the rest of the meal dipping our toasted bread in the dregs. My father, master of the kitchen, proceeded to tell her how to steam her own mussels (heavy on the white wine and garlic). We didn't have any bivalves to steam, but instead of making a pb&j for lunch my tween was attempting the sauce and had already lightly coated the sourdough with olive oil and toasted it. I told her where the wine was and then, questioning my own parenting, decided to check on things in person. I came home a few minutes later to find her chopping shallots and looking for truffle salt. So clearly, she grew out of her McDonalds chicken nugget phase (although occasionally she will ask me to hit the drive through for an apple pie...and I don't blame her...they are in fact delicious).

I am the last child. There is almost a decade between me and my oldest sibling. Everyone had long outgrown McDonalds by the time I learned about happy meals. My dad spent hours watching cooking shows and always kept a notebook and pencil by his chair to copy recipes. When I was small I'd order a dozen oysters on the halfshell. The waiters would ignore me, thinking it was a joke. I didn't know better. I was never allowed the palate of a child. My dad would yell, and eventually the waiters would bring out my oysters (and often a few other staff members to watch) while I quickly slurped them down. Sure they were slippery, but they tasted fresh and full of brine. Maybe a normal five-year-old would be ordering chicken nuggets, but instead I feasted on the ocean. I've never stopped. My own kids are likely to order sashimi, drive 30 miles for tacos from a gas station or comment on the bark of your brisket. Our palates are not exactly refined but they are broad.

I don't have a favorite food, I have dozens. I love a full-bodied cab or a rich Americano with oat milk. I love a brick oven-fired pizza with just the slightest crisp in the crust. I love the top crunchy part of a creme brulee. I think ossobuco is the ultimate comfort food, but so is Chick-fil-A macaroni and cheese. I think gnocchi are little happy pillows of deliciousness. I am the kind of person who has a favorite kind of olive (castelvetrano) and prefer to make my own salad dressing to anything that comes in a bottle. I love a steamed bao bun and believe that pho can cure a cold. Nothing hits better than a breakfast taco in a hand-made tortilla (hand made by someone else of course). Speaking of tortillas, I could eat an entire package of warm tortillas with or without honey and wash it down with a Topo Chico if my son hasn't drunk the last one. I could list food I love here for pages and pages, but the truth is I mostly love sharing it with others. I love a big rowdy table. I love a potluck as much as a fancy restaurant (maybe more). I love the bread and the wine, but I think what we love most about food is the community it creates and shares. I have not traveled the world (yet), but that won't stop me from tasting it.

Psalm 34:8 tells us to "taste and see that the Lord is good". I suppose there is no better sense to fully experience goodness than to taste it. I am always inspired by art, color and design. Music can calm me and help me focus or run faster, but food fills me up, evokes both memories and pleasure. Even when it is bad it is nourishing. Our bodies require it. We break bread in celebration and send casseroles in our condolences. Regardless of our situations, we all have to eat. No matter what you believe, we all want to be filled. A part of us always hungers, sometimes for food but most often for more.

Everyone in my house has their favorite celebratory meals or signature dishes. My husband makes a mean gumbo, my daughter is perfecting her scallion pancakes, my son can make a solid risotto, and I can cook most things, but please don't ask me to bake. One thing we have had to learn is how to work without our own constraints. When my son was in middle school he was diagnosed with celiac, and we've had to learn how to make many dishes without gluten.

MICHELLE HURST

Recently I've cut dairy, and I'm learning what I can eat or replace instead of getting hung up on what I can't. This week I made a pretty solid pesto even without the parm, and I have discovered where to get all the best non-dairy ice cream in a 15-mile radius. In other words, even with restrictions I am finding ways to taste and see what is still good instead of what is missing. It's not a bad reminder for the rest of my life.

I guess my daughter was correct in calling us a food family. It is one of the ways we explore and experience new things and new people. It is how we show care and celebrate each other. Some days it is just cereal for dinner but other days it is an abundance, but regardless we have the opportunity three times a day to taste and see. To remember. To say thank you.

If that doesn't make you hungry for something more, I don't know what will.

LAST FIRST DAY

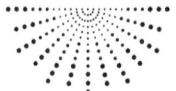

IN A FEW WEEKS, MY SON WILL START HIS SENIOR YEAR OF high school. I'll snap a photo in our foyer of his last first day. I no longer have to navigate the pickup line or worry whether someone will help him open his juice box. Instead, he will drive off and hopefully remember to charge his chrome book.

As his senior year approaches, I've been reflecting and remembering his first day of kindergarten.

A teacher myself, I was eager and relatively prepared for my son to start school (or so I thought). My son had been in preschool for years and was used to the routines. He could stand quietly in line, sit at a lunch table and print his name on the top line. Elementary school, however, felt different. The struggle felt less about the idea of him growing up, but I wrestled with the idea that from that day on my son would be receiving a grade. He'd be tested, ranked, scolded and compared.

We met his teacher a few days before school started. My son ran off in seconds with a friend from his soccer team and before we could stop them, they were both waist-deep into a big tub of Legos. I decided at that moment that he would be just fine, but I was not so sure about me. Suddenly sitting in that classroom with tiny chairs, I had a hundred questions. Incredibly basic ones, like how do I put money on his lunch ticket? Where am I supposed to buy that notebook on the list that I can't find at Walmart, Target or Staples? Where does he go in the mornings?

I also had questions that were less about what to do and more about my child's wellbeing. What if his teacher is mean? What if he never learns to listen and is always in trouble? What if he always forgets the number fourteen and never learns to count to twenty properly? Does his teacher know that he is left-handed and sometimes needs his inhaler? What if he can't put the straw in his Capri sun or zip his zipper by himself? Will someone tell him where to go after school? What if kids make fun of him for being little? What if he learns more bad words? What if he teaches his classmates the ones he already knows?

I worried that maybe I should have spent more time trying to teach him to read rather than letting him watch so many cartoons. At the very least, maybe I could have taught him how to tie his shoes and not given up and bought the dorky Velcro ones. If I let myself, I would have had a hundred more questions or what-ifs. And it all boiled down to one: will his teacher love my kid? Not, what kind of degree does she have? Nor, what fabulous lesson plans did she come up with? Not, how fun and warm and inviting her classroom looks! Or even, what is she doing to get him ready for the state standardized tests? But: will she see him? Will she encourage him? Will she love him?

As a high school teacher, I approached my own first day differently that year. My students filed in and I passed out the syllabi as usual. I showed funny video clips and did impressive science demonstrations. All day in the back of my mind, however, I thought about my little boy with his Lego backpack and Darth Vadar lunch box. I decided that my show could take a back seat to what was most important. Not lesson plans, cool demos, lunch schedules, parking permits, late work policies or even freshly ironed pants. I realized for the first time that all their mommas were sitting at home or at work hoping for me to love their kid. Hoping that I would see them and encourage them. Mommas want the exact same thing when their kid is six as when they are sixteen.

My son is now almost an adult, an adult who still occasionally forgets to brush his teeth and struggles to match his clothes. Still, he made it through kindergarten to become a kind, bright and funny seventeen-year-old. We've had twelve years of grades and tests and occasional folder signings. Now I know what to expect when I send him out the door.

He will learn calculus and how to hide from an active shooter.

He will apply for college and avoid the kids vaping in the bathroom.

He will forget his homework and find people to eat lunch with.

He will be ranked, but he will also be affirmed.

He will be challenged, he will be bored, and occasionally he will fail.

What I've learned is that there is an education in all three.

He is no longer the tiny five-year-old I dropped off, yet I can't help but hesitate sending him out the door. My questions have turned into hopes and prayers. I hope his teachers are qualified and not burned out from the last three difficult school years. I pray that they have substitutes when needed. I pray that our COVID boosters will do the trick. I pray that there isn't another shooting in our district this year. I pray that the teachers feel empowered and cared for.

One thing hasn't changed: I hope they see my kid. I hope they listen when he asks hard questions. I hope they can read his handwriting. I hope they laugh at his jokes.

Sure, I also hope they are good teachers, masters of their content, fast graders, strong communicators and great classroom managers.

But mostly, just like I asked when he was five, I hope they see and love my kid. I hope they can keep him safe. They might see a shaggy-haired almost adult who likely forgot to do his homework, but sometimes I still see a nervous five-year-old with a Lego backpack and a Star Wars lunch box.

CLAP OUT

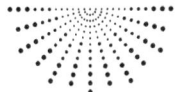

WE ARE QUICKLY APPROACHING GRADUATION IN OUR house. It is just over three weeks out, and I still have no idea how many tickets I will actually land. I have yet to order the tacos (because of course tacos) or purchase decorations.

I've been to more than my share of graduations. In addition to all the ones in my family, I taught high school for eighteen years. Often, I'd volunteer to be a line leader, and I'd walk on stage and sit with hundreds of graduates nervously pulling on their tassels or knee socks, praying not to trip as they walked across the stage, or trying to blow up a beach ball without me noticing.

Each year I listened to speech after speech encouraging them to move on. To go forth. To make a difference. To do something. The speeches were generally cliche but always earnest. Each time I listened, and I remembered my own high school graduation — occupying a seat like theirs in the G. Rollie White Coliseum, trying to spot my friends and family in that giant crowd. Then I also worried about not tripping across the stage. How my hair looked. Where I was going afterwards. As in the after-graduation party, not my future.

It would be another few months before I packed up my Grand Am and drove it seven hours north and west to an empty dorm with a potluck roommate. To a life where I knew no one. My bulletin boards, tiny closet and my now empty gas tank, all waiting to be filled with something new. My dad showed the RAs card tricks while I died from humiliation and hoped that this new girl I was going to share a closet with would like me OK. Or at least tolerate my James Dean posters and superior musical tastes. And not tell anyone that I occasionally snored.

At my own graduation, I did not listen to the speakers, or if I did, I can't remember what was said. I did not listen then, so I try to listen as an adult. Year after year of quotes and jokes and cliches that no longer apply. I can barely remember the girl I was. Sitting in the second-to-the-last row. But I am sure that someone stood on the stage and tried to tell her to go forth and make something of herself. That was almost twenty-five years ago, and I'm still working on the "making something of myself" part — but I did go. And it has been one of the best decisions I ever made. It feels very different, however, to think of my own son going.

Graduates are not the only ones that get attention at the end of the year. My district (and many others) celebrates fourth graders with a clap out as they leave elementary school and move on up to an intermediate campus. All the students line the halls, and the fourth graders take one last lap around the building. Many of them wear an elementary shirt signed by their classmates, and they feel big and special as they parade past the younger grades and prepare for things like switching classes and figuring out how to open a locker. At least three elementary schools filter into one intermediate school, and these kids will be mixed up with new classmates, choose electives and hopefully start wearing deodorant.

Last week the seniors in my district were all invited back to one of their twenty-four elementary campuses. Instead of youth sized t-shirts, this time they donned their college or military shirt under graduation robes. There is breakfast, slideshows, mascots, and old elementary yearbooks. It is no small thing; at my son's school, a hundred people filled the gym, including their old teachers, counselors, and principals. Even ones who have moved on to other campuses or cities. They recreate class photos and eat all the donuts and Chick-fil-A they possibly can before heading back to second period.

I watched seniors who needed to shave shelving picture books while waiting in the library. I saw surprise bloom on their faces as their elementary teachers remembered them. I saw students awkwardly find each other again. They'd grown apart over the years, but in the same gym as so many ho-downs and dodgeball games, they were reminded of their common history. Instead of upcoming AP exams, they talked about Cheetah bucks, lunch tables and field days.

Eventually, all the parents lined up and the almost graduates zipped up their robes. They ran the halls one last time. This time they were really as big as they had thought they were in the fourth grade. This time was really the last. This time they were really moving on, across the country and not just to the school a few miles down the street. This time their minds were on majors and deployments instead of combination lockers.

These next few weeks are full of senior events: awards, prom, senior night at church, and eventually my son will put on his robe again and find his seat on the stage during "Pomp and Circumstance." This time I will not be on stage; I will only be a spectator. Cheering wildly. This is the goal and the hope, but there is still a knot of loss in more than just my son's tassel.

Graduation seems like the cumulation and the bigger event, and maybe it will be. However, when I look at pictures from clap out, my heart feels like it is happening all at once. Like I should still be waiting in the pick-up line or trying to remember to sign his reading log. Graduation is the opportunity to celebrate an ending and an opportunity to look forward to what is next, but clap out was the rare opportunity to also remember exactly where he had been. I volunteered to help set up breakfast and was one of the first ones there. I saw each "kid" walk in, and they all said almost the exact same thing: "I remember this gym being so much bigger."

The room didn't change, but they did. The gym didn't shrink, they grew.

Sometimes we need to go back to where we started to see the difference.

It is a long journey. It goes on forever and is over in a blink.

DUCKS

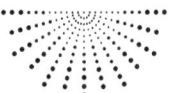

IT WAS A RISK, BUT I'D ORDERED ASSORTED AND GOOFY rubber ducks in bulk on Amazon. I knew I wanted to speak about being seen and where we find our worth and value.

I speak for a living. I'm good at it. I rarely get nervous anymore, even at big conferences. But it is one thing to talk about what you are an expert in, and another altogether to talk about the things your heart is still trying to figure out.

My friend Rhonda had used ducks to talk about healthy relationships to a group I lead. I was hoping I could apply the same analogy to how God values us. I got there a little early and spread out my ducks in the front. I talked about how God sees us and knows us. All of us, every hair and freckle and fault. *The very hairs of your head are all numbered. Don't be afraid; you are worth more than many sparrows.*[52]

I didn't have sparrows, but ducks were close enough. I told everyone to pick out a duck. Any duck. That it might be the most important decision they made all day. Eventually, the ducks were all accounted for. Next, I asked everyone to name their ducks, because of course their new friends would need a name. Lastly, I asked everyone to tell their neighbor three things about their duck.

In a matter of minutes, every duck had a name and a back story. Those plastic ducks had hobbies and ambitions and personality traits. One person asked to keep them. (I quietly exhaled, relieved that this wasn't going to completely flop). I offered someone on the front row a quarter for her duck.

She looked at me with pure disgust.

I told her everyone has a price and to name hers. I heard a few shouts from the crowd.

Anywhere from $5 to $25. Those ducks cost me just over a quarter each to buy, but in a matter of literally three minutes people were attached. Their ducks had increased in value because they had been chosen. They had been named. They were known. And now they seemed to be worth and valued at so much more than what I'd paid.

Our value is not in how we see ourselves or what we accomplish. Our worth is in the fact that God has chosen us. That He knows our names. That He searches us and knows us. Ephesians 1 tells us that we have been chosen and are adopted as sons (and daughters) by Jesus himself.[53] He paid the ultimate price on our behalf.

More often than not, if my change is only a few cents, I don't wait around long enough for the cashier to hand me my pennies. If change falls out of my pocket or purse, I occasionally don't bother to bend over to pick it up. Especially if it is just the copper variety. I know that they add up, but I still don't think that pennies are usually worth my time or effort to keep up with. I've heard rumors for a while now that the US Mint is going to stop making them. That we will have to start rounding up or down when paying in cash. This does not sound like any kind of loss to me. The reason, besides taking up all kinds of space at the bottom of my purse, turning green in my car's cup holder and the fact that you can't even use them in a vending machine, is that it actually costs 2.72 cents to make a penny.[54]

In other words, they cost more than they say they are worth.

A penny costs more than a penny.

Its worth is whatever someone decides to print right on the back, opposite Abe Lincoln. Its cost, however, is not decided but determined by what it's made of.

Pennies used to be made almost entirely of copper until copper got too expensive. Now they are made with cheaper metals and get just a thin copper plating. The world tends to look on the outside for worth rather than what is inside. It is easy to cover up the cheaper stuff with a thin varnish of what we really want others to see. What we try to sell others is the outside Instagrammed image through our most flattering filters, but what determines our worth goes deeper than that.

I have never been the kind of girl to balance a checkbook and have been known to raid my son's piggybank for change (or twenties). I have bounced a few checks, lost more debit cards than I can count, forgotten to pay the water bill and blown more than my share of pennies on things I do not really need.

I am bad with money.

But I am especially bad with the concept of worth.

Particularly my own.

I know what should be the truth. I know what the people I care about most would say. What the Bible says. What lots of other books say. But knowing something is true and feeling it aren't always the same. More often than not, I use the wrong standards and particularly the wrong internal dialogues. If a penny can be worth more than a penny — well, maybe I have been getting my own worth and value confused as well.

In other words, we have been getting it wrong. We have been looking in the wrong places for other people to tell us what things are worth. And of course when I use the word we, I mostly mean me.

Things that seem worthless are not lost in the eyes of our Father. It is not numbers of likes or bank accounts or pant sizes or GPAs or social media likes that determine value. It is not what people have told us. It is not, thankfully, even what we believe about ourselves.

Like a penny, our value comes from what we are made out of. More importantly, it comes from WHO made us. And made with such care that He takes the time to number every single hair on our head (and quite possibly even the ones that end up in the shower drain). Like for a rubber duck, it is in being chosen, named and known.

You are chosen. God knows your name.

You are worth more than many sparrows and pennies and ducks.

I KNOW

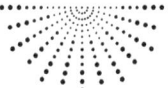

WHEN MY DAUGHTER HIT PUBERTY, SHE MOVED STRAIGHT into her room. It seemed dramatic and overnight, not a gradual release.

One day I can't get a minute alone and the next I hardly know she lives here, except for all the half-filled cups she leaves all over the house. One day she drones on and on about horses, youtubers, recess and pizza in the cafeteria and the next she answers with as few syllables as possible. I do my best to lure her out with the promise of her favorite foods or movies but mostly she retreats. Somedays I hear music and other days I hear power tools from behind her closed door. She rearranges. She paints her nails. She paints her furniture. She even occasionally does homework. She tries on new styles, friend groups and hair colors regularly. She has no idea who she is or wants to be.

I'm trying to give her the space to figure it out. Not so much space that she loses herself, but enough to find her own way rather than the one I might chart for her. She is pulling away, and it is a loss as much as it is a discovery.

Multiple times a week, I ask her to come downstairs. I ask her to watch a TV show with me or get an ice cream or coffee or sushi. I get mostly disinterest in return, but sometimes I land the occasional yes. I ask how her day was. Who made her laugh? What she learned in class or who she ate lunch with? Her answers are always short and concise. The compliments from her are rare; gone are the "best mom ever" notes I used to find. They have been replaced with long sighs and the occasional glare. Now when I hug her, she quickly brushes me off. It feels like rejection, but really it is becoming.

My son did the same at about her age, but my daughter has an edge and coolness that my son never showed. When I tell her goodnight or that I love her, she mostly just responds with, "I know," flat and full of nonchalance.

Unlike some of my friends, I do not hate this response. It doesn't feel like disrespect. To me, it provides an assurance. I could never have said that so casually at her age. Knowing I was loved took a lot longer for me to learn. I see her in all her angst, hormones and uncertainty and think if she knows that she is loved, she will be OK.

I've heard my friends talk about this inevitable withdrawal of their teens and read lamenting posts on social media. They mostly address how hurt the parent feels. Many parts of this teen thing are hard, but I see this part as normal. I see it as my job to keep asking. To show up as often as I can. I tell corny jokes and sing along to the radio. I say yes even when it is inconvenient. I try to slip a joke or sticker in her lunch, even though she tells me not to. I go thrift shopping with her, even though it makes me want to pull all my hair out. I am the one with a fully developed frontal cortex. I can handle a cold shoulder or permanently embedded earbuds. I am the one who keeps leaning in even as they pull slightly away.

Sometimes I miss when they used to smell of graham crackers and juice. I miss needy sticky hands reaching for mine. I do not, however, miss car seats or pick up lines or up-all-nights. This is the tradeoff. When they were young, I thought I'd never get to go to the bathroom or grocery store alone again, and now I have to practically beg them to sit next to me on the couch. Mothering a teenager is a continual practice in letting go.

I doubt I was a joy to live with at my daughter's age; I was headstrong, insistent and every bit as moody as my own teen. My mother, however, was always slightly distant. She did not respond to my teenage withdrawal with invitations and pursuit. She let me retreat. She loved me in the best ways she could, I just didn't always see it. Unlike my daughter, I grew up often not knowing. I constantly questioned my ability to be loved, wanted and seen.

My mother has improved much over the course of the year, but she is still struggling with memory issues and anxiety. I fear that I have missed the window for some conversations. She is fading, and so are our opportunities. These moments are hard but tender in their own way.

Recently I went home to visit and help after she was released from the hospital. Caretaking for a parent is every bit as draining and consuming as for a toddler. She argues as much as my teenage daughter over pills and meals and memories. Like mothering a teenager, caretaking is also a continual practice in letting go.

After a few days I was exhausted and desperate for my own bed. I had my car loaded and leaned in to give her a hug before heading back to my own family. I did not know how she would react. Sometimes she pulls away and refuses to be touched, but this time she accepted. She told me that she loved me; I smiled and responded, "I know."

NOT SO FIRM FOUNDATIONS

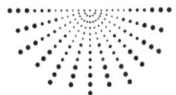

I KNOW HOW TO DO HARD THINGS. I HAVE A PRETTY SOLID track record. I've had brain surgery, gotten a doctorate, run half marathons and even occasionally managed to park straight on the first try. I've navigated illness, loss and messy relationships. I want to be the person who says that her hardships have made me stronger, made me better, and that I navigated all of them with grace.

However, that has not once been the case; every single time, I limped across the finish line. Some of those struggles have left a mark. I recently had someone assure me amid another hard thing that they were "solid" and could help me navigate this next thing. I was thankful for the stability to lean on, but another part of me shrank. I'm not sure I have ever felt solid in my whole life. I've often felt confident and capable; I believe in my own agency, and yet more often than I'd like, I still wobble.

On an especially wobbly day, after learning some complicated news paired with the loss of a former student, I go home physically shaking and overwhelmed. I have plans that I don't have the forethought to cancel. Weeks ago, I put the dinner with an old student on my calendar and, as I pull into the parking lot, I wonder if maybe this is a terrible idea. Once I was her physics teacher, and we've kept in touch over the last fifteen years. We've shared dinner, coffee, musical tastes and career advice over the decades. My current unsteadiness has me doubting my ability to be anyone's wise council, much less a fun dinner companion. I warn her before ordering that I am fresh out of wisdom or life advice for the day and she laughs, assuring me that I have doled out plenty over the years and tonight I can get a pass.

We talk about our mothers and steady partners and sorrow and soccer. I apologize for being such odd company, yet we still talk for hours. We are both honest and earnest and laugh loudly enough for the next table over to give us a side-eye. She tells me that her marriage is good (after a failed one), that her work is rewarding (after a career change), and that maybe she is happy for the first time. She smiles cautiously and tells me that "she is solid." I can only reply, "Oh no, there is that word again. It has been chasing me lately. I'm not sure I have ever been solid." She pays for both our dinners and promises me that from where she has been sitting, I always have been.

On the way home I silently list out the solid things and people in my life. It is not a short list. Even this day is full of them. I try to map out the right lines and boundaries before I go to sleep. I talk through some of it with my also solid husband. I tell him the parts that are too big and wonder what to do about them. Maybe if I tell enough people, I won't sink under the load.

I barely sleep, of course, despite the melatonin I swallowed. Eventually, I grab my headphones and click the Calm app on my phone. Multiple soundscapes and sleep meditations later, and I am no closer to sleep. Out of desperation, I try something slightly out of character. I type in a worship song title in my streaming service and listen to a dozen or so iterations of *Firm Foundations*[55] before my breathing settles and my heart calms.

It isn't all true for me. Sometimes I hate it when praise songs make promises that don't feel real. Or in the case of this song, promises that we've never been let down. I can tell you over and over the times I have cried out and gotten no response. No relief. No joy in chaos and no peace that makes no sense.

And yet, it is still where I reach. It is still a comfort to hear over and over that I won't go under, that I am held by strength. Held by something bigger than me. A story broader than a moment in a park or a hospital room or a funeral. It is still a promise I seek. Maybe a promise that I am in the middle of. It is still a promise that won't let me go.

My faith has never been solid. I've been stuck on that word all week. Maybe longer. And I worry that maybe that is the problem. I am not solid. I don't have a solid faith. I don't have a solid foundation. My vagabond heart will never get it right. I might be chasing after something solid, but sometimes what I really need is a soft place to land.

I find the verse about the wise man who built his house on a rock.[56] The one that could withstand the wind and rains and shaking. And in the middle of the night, with this song in my ear, I think maybe my definition of solid is too narrow.

Peter misinterpreted and misunderstood Jesus all the time. He tried to walk on water and sank. He argued about who was the greatest. Jesus rebuked him and called him a stumbling block. He told Jesus not to wash his feet. He fell asleep in the garden. He was the one who denied Jesus over and over and over. And yet he was the one who was restored. That was asked again and again and again.

Jesus called Peter the rock. The foundation for it all. If that is what it takes to be solid — Getting it wrong. Failure. Denial three times over — then maybe I am more solid than I think. Love and love and love. What can be more solid than that? It is one thing I am certain my heart can do. It is the rock on which I stand.

ACKNOWLEDGMENTS

I started writing these essays long before I ever imagined publishing a book. Over more than a decade, it has been shaped by countless relationships, experiences, and the encouragement of so many. I'm certain I have unintentionally left people out. Know that I often forget what I went to the grocery store to buy or where I put my keys, it isn't intentional. Know that I am still endlessly grateful. Your impact, whether mentioned here or not, is woven into these pages, and I couldn't have done it without you.

To my husband, an engineer by trade, but a maker at heart, who spends his time at Lowe's and in the garage, crafting things that matter to him. He sees this as my own version of making — and I'm grateful it involves less sanding. People don't always realize how much writing can cost, and though he's kept us on a budget, he's never stopped me from investing in my dreams. My kids – Writers are always afraid of running out of content, but loving my kids has at least taught me that love only expands. They give me plenty of content and make me want to be better. I'm proud of so many things, but none more than being your mom.

Growing up, my mother would never buy me the jeans I wanted, but she never hesitated to buy me books. I watched my father spend hours preparing to occasionally teach his Sunday School class with the same dedication as if he were studying for the MCAT. Perhaps this is where my love of learning and teaching stems from — but it also taught me that scripture can be questioned, pressed, and studied in depth.

I'm lucky enough to have found a church community that has always allowed space for questions and spotty attendance. My pastors and mentors have never made me feel less than or not good enough. Instead, they've listened, encouraged my voice, and even when we disagree, they remind me, "This is what we believe, but there is room to be wrong." To the teenagers I'm privileged to mentor each week — you let me pretend to lead, while really leading me. And to the Wesley Foundation, for giving me a faith that can be pressed, grow, and evolve instead of break. To my roommate who handed me books by Henri Nouwen and Brennan Manning and occasionally read my journals.

To my friend Tina H, who asked me to join a writing group a million years ago, when I didn't yet see myself as a writer. That group has long since folded, but each member offered me new perspectives and taught me that while writing might happen in a coffee shop, the real work happens in community. To my original writing cheerleaders — some close friends, some acquaintances, some strangers on the internet — who urged me forward: Amy D, Jennifer R, Dawn C, Kathleen H, Stephanie S, Anna S, Susan P, Peter J, Kim M, Alyssa J, Kathy C, Sharron H, Kay W, Erin F, Steph F, Beth G, and Kelly K, Kelly W to name just a few. For my quarters: Laura M, Rhonda R, Wendy T and Marie M.

Thank you to the professionals who led workshops, gave valuable coaching, and helped move me one step closer to publishing: Anne K, Mary D, Kristen V, and everyone who shared my work or posted encouragements along the way. My friend and fellow writer - Alanna M, for the final push that kept me going to the end. Special appreciation to Meggan and Lauren at Starfish Stories Publishing, for taking a chance on me and helping me navigate the path to making this book a reality.

To coffee shops, for giving me a space to write, type, and occasionally cry. To Spotify, for letting me create endless playlists, because everything in my life needs a soundtrack, especially writing. To the library, for offering me countless books for free, and to my camp friends, who understand a unique part of my heart. Especially to the one who is gone — no one would be prouder of me than her.

To my therapist, Susan R, who helped me find the courage to ask tough questions and tend to my own heart. I've been a writer long before I decided to do internal work or send her long unsolicited essays, but my writing changed because of the safe spaces she fostered. Every page here reflects her influence and work.

I'm grateful for the writers who taught me that faith and life don't come with "ten simple steps": Rachel Held Evans, Sarah Bessey, Lauren Winner, Kate Bowler, Tish Harrison Warren, Emily P. Freeman, Brené Brown, Glennon Doyle, Jen Hatmaker, Mary Laura Philpott, Kelly Corrigan, and Shauna Niequist. Anne Lamott, who showed me you can talk about Jesus and sometimes swear a little. For my friends and coworkers who kept telling this science girl that maybe she should write a book; for anyone who ignored my grammar or spelling in the process and for my high school English teachers, who, even though I never learned to diagram a sentence, did teach me how to fall in love with one. I'm forever thankful for the comfort of Mary Oliver, Americanos, Rory Gilmore and oversized sweatshirts. And finally, to anyone who gave me their email address, joined my mailing list, or clicked on an email — thank you for believing in my words and remaining with me.

ABOUT THE AUTHOR

Dr. Michelle Hurst is a wife, mother of two, writer, and science educator based in Texas. Her work has been featured in The Mighty, Grown and Flown, and (in)Courage. She writes with warmth and authenticity about faith, chronic illness, hope, relationships, and middle age. A lover of coffee, tea, wine, books, and quiet hikes, Michelle finds joy in life's small, ordinary moments while embracing its complexities with honesty and hope.

You can connect with Michelle on her website at: www.michellewallishurst.com or through email at michelle@michellewallishurst.com

ALSO BY MICHELLE HURST

Essays Previously Published

Last First Day previously published at Grown & Flown

Store Bought and Good and Beautiful Things previously published at (in)Courage

Take Courage previously published at Her View From Home

Door Frames, New Shoes, Last, Quarters, Different and I Know posted in part at Grit and Grace Project

PART IV
NOTES

PART I
PART 1 STUBBORN FAITH

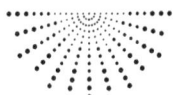

1. Romans 8:28 (NIV). And we know that in all things God works for the good of those who love him, who have been called according to his purpose.
2. Hebrews 11:1 (NIV). Now faith is confidence in what we hope for and assurance about what we do not see.
3. Ephesians 3:17-19 (TLB).
4. "Here are the two best prayers I know: "Help me, help me, help me," and "Thank you, thank you, thank you." - Anne Lammott, Traveling Mercies, Some Thoughts on Faith.
5. Psalm 17:6 (NIV)
6. Bell, Rob. *Drops Like Stars: A Few Thoughts on Creativity and Suffering*. HarperOne, 2009.
7. Bolz-Weber, Nadia. "Seeing the Underside and Seeing God: Tattoos, Tradition, and Grace." *On Being*, Krista Tippett, 15 Apr. 2021, onbeing.org/programs/nadia-bolz-weber-seeing-the-underside-and-seeing-god-tattoos-tradition-and-grace/.

8. Hebrews 13:8 (NIV)
9. Genesis 18:27 (NIV)
10. Tyson, Neil deGrasse. *Astrophysics for People in a Hurry*. W.W. Norton & Company, 2017.
11. Psalm 113:3 (NIV)
12. "My Faith Walk: Ordinary Time." *My Faith Walk*, www.myfaithwalk.org/ordinary-time. Accessed 1 Oct. 2024.
13. Hillsong United. "Oceans (Where Feet May Fail)." *Zion*, Hillsong Music, 2013.
14. Voskamp, Ann. *One Thousand Gifts: A Dare to Live Fully Right Where You Are*. Zondervan, 2010.
15. Bessey, Sarah. "Advent Is for the Ones Who Know Longing." *Sarah Bessey*, Substack, 29 Nov. 2021. https://sarahbessey.substack.com/p/advent-is-for-the-ones-who-know-longing. Accessed 1 Oct. 2024.
16. "O Holy Night." *The Celebration Hymnal: Songs and Hymns for Worship*, Word Music, 1997
17. Parker, Nick. "Why Are We So Obsessed with True Crime?" *Science Focus*, 24 Oct. 2023, www.sciencefocus.com/the-human-body/why-are-we-so-obsessed-with-true-crime.
18. Bishop, Angela. "Why Art, Chekhov, and Questions with No Answers." *The Burg*, 24 Aug. 2023, theburgnews.com/culture/why-art-chekhov-and-questions-with-no-answers.
19. Matthew 15.
20. John 21:15-19

PART 2 RECKLESS HOPE

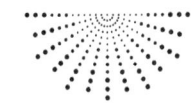

- 21. Hebrews 10:23
- 22. Palmer, Amanda. *The Art of Asking: How I Learned to Stop Worrying and Let People Help*. Grand Central Publishing, 2014.
- 23. Ecclesiastes 3:1
- 24. Exodus 14:14, NIV.
- 25. 2 Corinthians 12:9-11, NIV.
- 26. Sexton, Anne. "Courage." *The Complete Poems*, Houghton Mifflin, 1999.
- 27. Joshua 1:9
- 28. Matthew 14:27
- 29. Powers, Richard. *The Overstory*. W.W. Norton & Company, 2018.
- 30. "Trees and Shrubs." *Manzanar National Historic Site*, National Park Service, www.nps.gov/muwo/learn/nature/treesandshrubs.htm.
- 31. Miranda, Lin-Manuel. "Wait for It." *Hamilton: An American Musical*, Atlantic Records, 2015.

- 32. Brown, Brené. "Brené on Comparative Suffering, the 50/50 Myth, and Settling the Ball." *Unlocking Us*, 1 Apr. 2020, brenebrown.com/podcast/brene-on-comparative-suffering-the-50-50-myth-and-settling-the-ball/.
- 33. 1 Corinthians 10:13
- 34. Cisneros, Sandra. *The House on Mango Street*. Vintage Books, 1991.
- 35. Romans 5:3-5, NIV.
- 36. Isaiah 40:31, KJV
- 37. Isaiah 40:31, NIV
- 38. "Silent Night." *The Celebration Hymnal: Songs and Hymns for Worship*, Word Music, 1997.

PART II
PART 3 ORDINARY LOVE

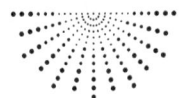

- 39. *Jerry Maguire*. Directed by Cameron Crowe, Columbia Pictures, 1996.
- 40. 1 John 4:19, NIV
- 41. 1 John 4:12
- 42. Burgess, Matthew. *Enormous Smallness: A Story of E. E. Cummings*. Illustrated by Kris Di Giacomo, Enchanted Lion Books, 2015
- 43. Stone, Elizabeth. "It is to decide forever to have your heart go walking around outside your body." *The New York Times*, 6 Nov. 1994.
- 44. Capone, Al. "Be careful who you call your friends. I'd rather have four quarters than 100 pennies." *Goodreads*, www.goodreads.com/quotes/140695-be-careful-who-you-call-your-friends-i-d-rather-have-four.
- 45. Oliver, Mary. "The Summer Day." *New and Selected Poems*, Beacon Press, 1992.
- 46. Oliver, Mary. "The Journey." *Dream Work*, Atlantic Monthly Press, 1986.

- 47. Oliver, Mary. "A Poetry Handbook." *A Poetry Handbook: A Prose Guide to Understanding and Writing Poetry*, Harcourt Brace, 1994.
- 48. Oliver, Mary. "In Blackwater Woods." *New and Selected Poems*, Beacon Press, 1992.
- 49. Oliver, Mary. "Wild Geese." *Dream Work*, Atlantic Monthly Press, 1986.
- 50. "Why Do Geese Fly in a V?" *Library of Congress*, www.loc.gov/everyday-mysteries/zoology/item/why-do-geese-fly-in-a-v/.
- 51. Jackson, Anne. *Permission to Speak Freely: Essays and Art on Fear, Confession, and Grace*. Thomas Nelson, 2010.
- 52. Luke 12:7, NIV
- 53. Ephesians 1:3-5
- 54. "U.S. Penny Costs More to Make Than It's Worth." *Money Digest*, 22 Sept.2023,www.moneydigest.com/1513982/penny-costs-more-to-make-than-worth/#:~:text=In%202022%2C%20the%20United%20States,zinc%20for%20the%20price%20increase.
- 55. Carnes, Cody, and Chandler Moore. *Firm Foundation (He Won't)*. LIFT Worship and Capitol CMG Publishing, 2021.
- 56. Matthew 7:24

DIGITAL ACCOMPANYING STUDY GUIDE

Grab the digital accompanying study guide for free right here: